The Great Book of Black Heroes

30 Fearless and Inspirational
Black Men and Women that Changed History

Bill O'Neill

ISBN: 978-1-64845-072-3

ON'T FORGET YOUR FREE BOOKS

CONTENTS

INTRODUCTION

Welcome to *The Great Book of Black Heroes: Thirty Black Men and Women Who Have Impacted History*! As the title indicates, this is a book that focuses on 30 of the most memorable and impacting men and women of African descent in history. Read through these pages and delve into the fascinating and gripping lives of these people in 30 engaging chapters that conclude with a "Did you know?" section that lists five facts about each individual. Although this book is 100% fact-based and designed to make you a more knowledgeable person, it is so much more than a boring history or social studies book. As you read through this book, the lives of these heroes - some long-dead - will come alive and speak to you as if they were in the room with you!

You probably already know a little about some important African-American personalities, but this book covers some of who are considered the greatest Black heroes not just from the United States, but also Latin America, the Caribbean, and Africa. Yes, you will read about the profiles of such Black American luminaries as Martin Luther King Junior, Frederick Douglass, and Redd Foxx, but you'll also be introduced to some people you've probably never heard of, such as Jomo Kenyatta, Gaspar Yanga, and Kaleb of Axum.

And this book is not just confined to current or modern leaders.

The history of Black heroes stretches back into ancient times. Taharqa was an ancient Nubian king who ruled over a vast empire in the 7th century BCE and was even mentioned in the Bible! Other impactful Black heroes from history profiled in this book include Toussaint L-Ouverture, who is sometimes called the "Black George Washington," and Shaka, the king of the mighty Zulu people in South Africa.

If you're wondering about Black heroines, don't worry - this book has plenty.

We'll explore the lives of some pretty phenomenal Black women who left as big an impact as their male counterparts in politics and entertainment, proving that women are just as capable as men.

So, sit back, relax, and get ready to embark on a journey that will bring across multiple continents and through thousands of years of history. You are sure to learn quite a bit, but I guarantee that you'll also have some fun in the process!

CHAPTER 1

HAILE SELASSIE: A MODERN BLACK EMPEROR

The eastern African nation of Ethiopia is truly a unique place that in many ways stands apart from its neighbors - or all of Africa, for that matter. Besides Liberia, it is the only African nation that was never colonized by European powers and its rich history goes back more than 2,000 years. The oldest form of writing in sub-Saharan Africa was developed in Ethiopia (known until fairly recently as Abyssinia) and is still in use.

Plus, the country is full of ancient monuments that testify to its early importance.

Some of Christianity's earliest churches and monasteries can be found in Ethiopia and other signs of Ethiopia's ancient greatness are abundant. Modern Ethiopians are well-aware of their country's rich history, especially their former rulers' connection to the biblical Solomon.

If you're familiar with the Old Testament, then you know that King Solomon of Israel was believed to have been one of the wisest men in the world.

But Solomon was also a ladies' man.

Among the possibly hundreds of wives and concubines Solomon had (how he had time to be the world's wisest man is anyone's guess!), was the Queen of Sheba. Although modern scholars aren't sure where Sheba was born, the people of medieval Ethiopia believed it was in their country.

So began the tradition that the Ethiopian monarchy was descended from King Solomon. The Ethiopian ruling house became known as the Solomonic Dynasty and its rulers were known as emperors.

The most famous and influential of all the Solomonic emperors was Haile Selassie.

Born into Royalty

Today, Ethiopia is a poor country as the result of decades of civil war and famine, but for centuries it was the jewel in the crown of Africa in terms of money, power, and prestige. While much of Africa was being colonized by the European powers, or in North Africa, by the Ottoman Empire, Ethiopia developed independently and was even afforded a level of respect most nations never gave to the rest of Africa.

This was the world Lij Tafari Makonnen was born into on July 23, 1892.

Lij, who would later become Haile Selassie, when he ascended to the throne, was born into the Ethiopian royal family and therefore a life of privilege and influence. He was tutored privately, receiving a standard academic education as well as a crash course in military tactics, government administration, and the rough and tumble nuances of African politics.

Lij's father died in 1906, but it didn't stop the young man's ascent within the Ethiopian government. He married a well-connected woman, served as governor of a province, and became a central player in the highest levels of government. When the ruling emperor converted to Islam in 1916, the military deposed him and replaced him with Empress Zewditu. She then gave Lij the title *Ras*, which was essentially the role of co-regent.

Lij's name was then Ras Tafari. You've probably heard that term before in reference to dreadlocked, weed-smoking guys from Jamaica, right? Well, the connection between them and Haile Selassie began at this point, but we'll get to that in a bit.

Influencing the World

Tafari traveled throughout Europe in the 1920s, extending an olive branch to all who would accept, but making it clear that Abyssinia would never be colonized.

But Tafari soon realized that he had more pressing issues to deal with back home.

Although Ethiopia was wealthier and more politically stable at that time than most of post-colonial Africa would be later, it still had plenty of court intrigues. Tafari's ambition raised the ire of the empress and others in the royal court. They tried to remove him, but he together with his loyal cadre of military followers defeated his opponents. The empress made him *negus* (king) in 1928, and when she died in 1930, he became Emperor Haile Selassie.

Rule is often a heavy burden on those who accept or take it up, especially in unstable regions and times, which was no exception in Selassie's case.

In 1935, in the lead up to World War II, Ethiopia was invaded and occupied by fascist Italy. Selassie urged his people to resist but was forced into exile in 1936, spending much of the war in England. It was during this time that Selassie became a well-known international celebrity, using his charm and charisma to influence the leaders of the most powerful nations to support him.

After Ethiopia was liberated in 1941, Selassie returned to his country and immediately set out to modernize his nation.

Ethiopia was the first African nation to join the United Nations and in 1963, Selassie was the leading figure in the formation of the Organization of African Unity.

Things weren't always easy for Selassie. He had to battle famines and was often accused of violating political dissidents' human rights, but by the late 1960s, most people in the world — which included the Western, communist, and Non-Aligned states - viewed Selassie as a thoughtful, reasonable leader, and Ethiopia as an example of what the other newly-independent African nations could be.

But what about that Rastafarian thing?

Rastafarianism as it is known today was the result of different political and religious ideas that converged in the 1930s. Essentially, Rastafarianism philosophy combined various Christian revivalist teachings, Afrocentrism that sometimes bordered on Black supremacist ideas, and a belief that marijuana use is not only biblically sanctioned, but a sacrament. Rastafarians pointed to biblical passages that mentioned Ethiopia as proof that the country was their homeland, much as Israel was for Jewish people.

Despite most Jamaicans being descended from West African tribes that were quite differently ethnically and culturally from Ethiopians, the movement caught on there by the 1960s, with many Rastafarians believing Halie Selassie was the second coming of Christ.

When Selassie made an official state visit to Jamaica in 1966, Rastafarianism became even more popular.

When reporters asked Selassie if he believed he was god, he always answered clearly that he was a Christian and was only a man. Still, he never disparaged others for their beliefs and instead tried to converted Rastafarians to the Ethiopian Orthodox Church.

Haile Selassie remained quite popular for a monarch throughout the world and at home into the 1970s, but famine led to a severe economic and political crisis in 1974. A communist revolution brought the emperor's government down, and the royal family was imprisoned in September 1974.

On August 28. 1975, the new government announced that Selassie had died in prison from respiratory failure, although to this day, many believe that the emperor's breathing problems were caused by assassins who strangled him.

Although the communists extinguished the Solomonic Dynasty in Ethiopia, they could not erase the legacy of Haile Selassie as a patriot, diplomat, and Black hero for millions of people around the world.

DID YOU KNOW?

- Selassie's supporters were not allowed to give him a proper, Christian burial until the communist regime fell in 1991. Although the Ethiopian government finally did so in 2000, many believe that the bones interred in the grave do not belong to the emperor.

- Selassie and his wife had six children.

- When Selassie opened Ethiopia to the world in the 1950s and '60s, it proved to be a double-edged sword. Selassie became incredibly popular with world leaders and citizens of other countries due to his travels, but many Ethiopians adopted Marxist, communist, and anti-monarchy ideas when they studied in Europe and North America.

- The Italian army quickly overwhelmed the Ethiopian army in 1935, but resistance continued. Haile Selassie's cousin, Imru, led the guerilla group known as the Black Lions against the Italian occupation.

- The women of Halie Selassie's family were finally released from prison in 1989 and the men in 1990. Most eventually resettled in England and the United States.

CHAPTER 2

THOMAS SOWELL:
BLACK AND CONSERVATIVE

The United States is a country rich with a diversity of opinions and ideas. Beyond the standard "liberal" and "conservative" appellations there are also libertarians, populists, socialists, and any number of combinations of two or more of these ideologies. Truly, America is a country where a person can believe what he or she wants and can take those beliefs on the campaign trail and to the ballot box.

With that said, Americans, like all people, still have their prejudices. When it comes to politics, many people still think that only certain groups should, or can, follow certain ideologies.

Only poor people vote Democrat.

Only rich people vote Republican.

And all Black people are Liberal Democrats.

But in America, assumptions are meant to be challenged and antiquated rules are often broken, so in the late 1960s, when the Civil Rights movement was at its peak, a young Black economist named Thomas Sowell challenged many assumptions on race and politics. As Sowell made a name for himself during the 1970s and '80s, he endeared himself to many American political conservatives, while earning the ire of the left wing of the political spectrum. Through it all, Thomas Sowell became a great American thinker, paving the way for later important Black conservatives, and proving the adage that you can't judge a book by its cover.

Learning Self Sufficiency

It would be an understatement to say that, when Thomas Sowell was born on June 30, 1930 in Gastonia, North Carolina, he wasn't given a winning hand. Sowell's father died before he was born, his mother was too poor to care for him so he was raised by an aunt, and of course, segregation was the law of the land in North Carolina at that time. Things began to change for young Sowell, though, when he moved with his family to New York City at the age of nine.

Although New York didn't have the same legal segregation that Sowell had experienced in North Carolina, there was still an unwritten yet always enforced type of segregation. Sowell quickly learned that there were neighborhoods he couldn't enter and jobs he would never have. Still, Thomas decided to do whatever he could to better his position in life.

He served in the Korean War in the United States Marine Corp and entered college upon his return home. Like many people of all races and backgrounds, Sowell's college experience would help define who he would become: a professional academic.

From Marx to Friedman

No matter the country or the era, college campuses tend to be hotbeds of left-wing thought. When Thomas Sowell entered the historically Black College of Howard University in the 1950s, he was attracted to left-wing ideas, and this was bolstered by the left-wing worldview of the university.

Sowell later wrote that he was a dyed in red Marxist during his early college years.

Sowell's turn to Marxism was to be expected. It was obvious to everyone who knew him that he was a bright young man, but the specter of segregation and discrimination always loomed over any of his accomplishments. The fact that he was born poor also contributed to Sowell flirting with Marxism, but by the time he entered Harvard and graduated with a BA in economics from the prestigious university in 1958, his political journey had taken him full circle to conservatism.

Thomas Sowell had given up on Marxism and embraced the ideas of Chicago School economists such as Milton Friedman.

Yes, he was born poor and surrounded by discrimination, but Sowell was also taught to be self-sufficient. He also believed that, despite its problems, the United States was the best nation on Earth and that the best way for Black Americans to be successful was through economic freedom and empowerment.

Across the years, Sowell has taught economics at numerous universities in the 1970s and '80s; authored scores of books on economics, race, and politics; held many government and official positions; and appeared on numerous radio, television, and Internet shows to promote his ideas and debate his detractors. Throughout it all, Sowell has been unapologetic as he offered his often scathing assessment of liberal ideas.

"The black family survived centuries of slavery and generations of Jim Crow," Sowell wrote "but it has disintegrated in the wake of the liberals' expansion of the welfare state."

Sowell often managed to turn off the mainstream of Black American civil rights activists, but he has inspired the still relatively small but constantly growing number of Black conservatives.

South Carolina Republican Senator Tim Scott, former US Congressman Allen West, former presidential candidate Alan Keyes, conservative activist Candace Owens, former NFL player Hershel Walker, and countless others can all trace their political lineage to a certain degree back to Thomas Sowell.

As much as Thomas Sowell is a political hero to conservative Americans of all races, he will continue to be even more so for the growing number of conservative Black Americans.

DID YOU KNOW?

- Sowell was initially not in favor of Donald Trump's presidency; instead, he supported Texas Senator Ted Cruz. Later he stated that he voted for and supported Trump.

- Due to his strong advocacy of *laissez-faire* economics, Sowell has found his greatest support among the libertarian wing of the Republican Party.

- After earning his BA at Harvard, Sowell would later earn a MA at Columbia and a Ph.D. from the University of Chicago, which is where he became acquainted first-hand with economist Milton Friedman and the philosophy known as the "Chicago School" of economics.

- Sowell has been married twice and has two children.

- Sowell wrote syndicated columns that were published in several prominent newspapers and magazines for most of his adult life. He finally retired from writing the columns in 2016 at the age of 86. Now that's an intellectual ironman!

CHAPTER 3

TOUSSAINT L'OUVERTURE: LEADING HAITI AGAINST NAPOLEON

When the nation that would become the United States of America attained its independence from Great Britain in 1783 through a hard-fought war and support by the French and Spanish, it set into motion a series of unstoppable events in the Americas. The Spanish colonies, led by men such as Simón Bolivar of Venezuela, began breaking away in the early 1800s and Brazil declared its independence from Portugal in 1822.

New nation-states formed throughout North America and South America that for the most part are the countries that exist on those continents today.

The Caribbean nations, though, were in a somewhat different situation.

Most of the Caribbean islands were ruled by the British, although the French, Spanish, and Dutch had their share of colonies as well, and unlike the mainland of the Americas, large scale European settlement never took place. The vast majority of the population of the Caribbean islands were Black Africans, who the rulers wanted to keep in a servile, compliant status.

But by the late 1700s, things were changing throughout the world.

The Enlightenment challenged the very idea of slavery and the American Revolution seemed to be a signal to everyone in the Americas, regardless of their race, to rise and take their freedom by force if need be.

This general period of lofty philosophical ideals and political upheavals led to the very violent and bloody French Revolution (1789-1799), which was supposed to bring a utopian government to France. Instead, it allowed Napoleon Bonaparte, arguably the modern world's first dictator, to come to power.

Napoleon then proceeded to conquer most of continental Europe, while his primary enemy, Great Britain, picked away at French colonies around the world.

One of those colonies was Saint-Domingue.

In the big picture of the Napoleonic Wars (1803-1815), Saint-Domingue wasn't very important. It was a relatively small French colony that shared the island of Hispaniola with the Spanish colony of Santo Domingo. Today, those two colonies are the independent countries of Haiti and the Dominican Republic, respectively.

Saint-Domingue was a sugar-producing colony that was home to about 40,000 French citizens, nearly 30,000 mulattoes, and almost 500,000 Black slaves who were mainly within a generation of being from Africa. Conflicts between the groups were common and in 1791, major slave revolts broke out across the colony. These threatened to turn into a race war that could extinguish the White and mulatto populations.

The British and Spanish saw an opportunity at that point and began sending arms and men to support the massive slave revolt, but the problem was that the rebellion had no true leader.

No true leader...until Toussaint L'Ouverture stepped forward.

L'Ouverture was an educated slave with a keen sense of military tactics and a charisma that allowed him to unify most of the slaves of Saint-Domingue under his leadership. Eventually, after a series of tough battles and several massacres, L'Ouverture successfully drove the French out of Saint-Domingue to create the free nation-state of Haiti.

For his efforts, Toussaint L'Ouverture is remembered by people around the world as one of the earliest Black freedom fighters in the modern world.

Finding His Way

Because L'Ouverture was born into slavery in Saint-Domingue, many of the details of his early life remain a mystery. Some historians believe he was born as early as 1739, while others give a later date of 1746. Regardless of when L'Ouverture was born, the reality is that he was born into a truly difficult situation, to say the least.

Slavery in the Americas was inhumane and often brutal, though its severity varied from colony to colony. In Saint-Domingue, a complex racial hierarchy developed in which a sizable number of mulattos came to enjoy privileges that were off-limits to even Black freedmen, which caused resentment in the colony that often led to violence.

Saint-Domingue's Black slaves were therefore often treated much more harshly than in other places in the Americas, being subjected to violence regularly and usually denied even standard educations.

But young L'Ouverture had the benefit of having an educated, freedman godfather who was willing to impart his knowledge to him. L'Ouverture learned how to read and write French, in addition to his native Creole, and became familiar with Enlightenment philosophers. Also, his father, who was from Africa, taught him traditional medicine and herbal lore, which he would later find beneficial during his years as a military commander.

It is believed that in 1777 L'Ouverture was freed, allowing him to pursue several business ventures.

By 1791, when the Haitian Revolution began, L'Ouverture had amassed a small fortune, owning at least one plantation and several slaves. He was a respected figure in Saint-Domingue among freedmen, mulattos, and Whites and could've just sat back and enjoyed his fortune.

Instead, L'Ouverture decided to risk it all by becoming a revolutionary.

A Politician on the Battlefield

The Haitian Revolution began, and ended, as an especially brutal affair where the Black slaves targeted the colony's White and Mulatto population for extermination. The years in between, though, were marked by a series of conventional military battles, combined with some guerilla activity led by L'Ouverture.

During the first five years of the Haitian Revolution, the former slaves of the colony were led by L'Ouverture, who was largely funded by the Spanish and British. The Spanish and British hoped to use the rebellion to their advantage by diminishing the French Empire, although neither nation wanted to see the widespread emancipation of slaves in the region.

L'Ouverture demonstrated leadership abilities on the battlefield that amazed his friends and foes alike. After all, many at the time wondered, "How could a Black man, never mind a former slave, be such a good commander?"

Well, part of the reason for L'Ouverture's success was his charisma, which allowed him to always replenish his numbers.

L'Ouverture also had a keen political sense, which was demonstrated when he turned against the Spanish in 1794.

After declaring war against Spain, L'Ouverture led the conquest of the entire island of Hispaniola in 1801, much to the chagrin of Napoleon.

L'Ouverture then formulated a constitution that—aside from abolishing slavery—was quite conservative. The constitution recognized that Saint-Domingue was still a French colony and that Napoleon was the head-of-state, although all Haitians were to be recognized as French citizens. The Catholic Church would be the State religion and L'Ouverture was to be governor dictator, essentially for life.

This was all too much for Napoleon, who sent troops to retake Saint-Domingue in early 1802.

But L'Ouverture had a plan to resist the French. He was smart enough to know that his army was not equipped or trained well enough to defeat the French head-on, so he ordered his men to retreat to the interior, where yellow fever would hopefully aid in the resistance.

The fighting was tough but in the end, it wasn't a French bullet that got L'Ouverture.

On May 22, 1802, Jean-Jacques Dessalines, one of L'Ouverture's most trusted officers and the future first leader of independent Haiti, betrayed the general to the French. The exact details of the betrayal are still a bit fuzzy, but the result was that L'Ouverture was arrested and extradited to France where he died in prison on April 7, 1803.

The exact details of L'Ouverture's death are also hazy and somewhat of a mystery of history.

What isn't a mystery, though, is the impact L'Ouverture had on freedom movements in the Americas and beyond. Word of L'Ouverture's quickly spread throughout the world, making him an icon of Black freedom.

DID YOU KNOW?

- In addition to his strategic capabilities, L'Ouverture demonstrated diplomatic skills many times in his life. He negotiated a treaty with the British in 1798 and also a trade treaty with the United States that year.

- L'Ouverture married and had two sons with his wife, Suzanne, although he claimed to have many more illegitimate children with multiple wives.

- Although the Haitian Revolution was preceded by the rebels conducting several Voodoo ceremonies, there is no evidence that L'Ouverture took part in any of those, as he was a devout Roman Catholic.

- L'Ouverture's birth name was François Dominique Toussaint. In 1793 he added "L'Ouverture," which is French for "opening," as he was quite proficient at finding the openings in his enemies' formations.

- The Haitian Revolution was the largest slave uprising in the world since the Third Servile War (73-71 BCE) and was the only successful slave revolt in the Americas.

CHAPTER 4

PELÉ: THE WORLD'S MOST POPULAR ATHLETE

In a world where people are often divided over politics, race, class, and any other number of issues that are either real or imagined, sports may often bring us together. Whether it's playing catch with your kids, getting a pickup game of basketball or football (American or otherwise) together with your neighbors, or watching your favorite team at the local sports bar, sports can often transcend many of our differences, even if just temporarily.

And in the history of sports there have been many athletes who have overcome those barriers to bring fans of all backgrounds together under one banner.

Wayne Gretzky is perhaps the most recognized and universally-loved hockey player in history, and few people around the world don't know who Michael Jordan is or respect the man and the player that he was. But few would argue that the most recognized and popular athlete of all-time is the Black Brazilian football (soccer if you're in North America or Australia) player Edson Arantes do Nascimento.

You might be thinking, "Who's Edson Arantes do Nascimento?", which is understandable, but chances are you know him by his mononym nickname, Pelé.

Pelé became famous for his feats on the pitch, which involved plenty of fancy footwork, agility, power, and at times seemingly gravity-defying moves that helped him score an incredible 1,281 goals in 1,363 FIFA sanctioned professional club matches and 77 goals for the Brazilian national team in 92 games. He led Brazil to three World Cup Championships and is credited with being one of the reasons for the phenomenal increase in popularity of soccer in the United States when he played for the New York Cosmos of the now-defunct North American Soccer League from 1975 to 1977.

Pelé was the highest-paid athlete in the world for a time and even had an Atari game named after him.

But just as important as the impact Pelé made on the football pitch, he has been a lifelong advocate for the poor in Brazil and is known for his generosity and class.

Football As an Escape

Edson Arantes do Nascimento was born on October 23, 1940 to a working poor family in the Minas Gerais state of Brazil. Due to a lack of job prospects, Edson's father moved the family to the city of Bauru in the state of São Paulo. Life wasn't easy for Edson and his two siblings; luxuries were rare in the home, but it wasn't quite the favela (slum).

Plus, Edson's father, Dondinho, was a decent football player who had some success in the lower leagues of Brazilian professional football. So, Pelé spent countless hours with his father learning the basics of the game before he developed a unique style of his own.

It didn't take long for him to "become" Pelé.

The origin of the nickname Pelé remains somewhat of a mystery. Pelé himself claims to not know its origins, while others believe it had something to do with his mispronunciation of a word. Whatever the case, by the time Pelé was in his teens, it was clear that he had a natural gift for the game. Combining that with his father's training, he was well on his way to a lucrative professional career.

Becoming an International Superstar

It would be an understatement to say that Pelé's rise to the top of the sports world was meteoric. In 1956, at the tender age of 15, Pelé's amateur coach brought him for a tryout with the professional team Santos Football Club. The Santos coaches were so impressed with the young man that they gave him a professional contract on the spot.

One year later, Pelé was leading the Brazilian national team and in 1958, he won his first World Cup Championship.

A large part of the reason why Pelé is considered one of history's greatest Black heroes is how he conducted himself throughout his life. Today, it's common — or almost expected — for professional athletes to be involved in drug and/or criminal scandals. Although Pelé wasn't a saint and had a notable weakness for women (he was married three times and had several affairs), he was never involved in criminal or drug activity.

And Pelé scored all his goals without the help of performance-enhancing drugs!

Another thing that sets Pelé apart from many professional athletes today is his loyalty. Professional players in all major sports leagues routinely leave their teams for bigger contracts, and in football, players even often leave their countries for more pay. The top Brazilian players today usually play in higher-paying European professional leagues, which means the only chance most of their fans have of seeing them in person is in the national team games played in Brazil.

But Pelé stayed loyal to Santos and his Brazilian fans. Some of the biggest clubs in Europe offered Pelé contracts that Santos, or any club in Brazil, could not match, yet he decided to stay with Santos for 19 seasons.

After his 19th season, he decided to sign a contract with the New York Cosmos and was amazed at the reception that Americans gave him. Pelé was invited to the White House by President Nixon, he promoted an array of products in commercials, and fans filled stadiums to see the Brazilian superstar work his magic on the pitch. In fact, without Pelé the NASL probably would've become defunct much sooner.

After his stint in the NASL, Pelé retired to his native Brazil as a national hero. But more importantly, Pelé transcended race and nationality to become a global phenomenon and a hero to millions, which makes him one of the greatest Black sports heroes in history.

DID YOU KNOW?

- In another example of how Pelé transcended divisions, the warring factions in the Nigerian Civil War agreed to a ceasefire to allow the people to watch Pelé play in a 1969 exhibition game in Lagos, Nigeria.

- Pelé's final game is regarded by many as one of the most incredible events in sports history. The game was between the New York Cosmos and Santos FC at a sold-out Giant's Stadium. Before the game, Pelé addressed the stadium, saying "Love is more important than what we can take in life." He played the first half for the Cosmos, scoring the final goal of his career, and the second half for Santos. The final score was 2-1 New York.

- Pelé popularized football's moniker "the beautiful game" in the 1960s, although the term had been around earlier.

- An interesting aspect of Pelé's life is his political views or lack thereof. Brazil's right-wing military dictatorship suspected him of sympathizing with those on the radical left in the 1970s, while more recently some on the left have accused the superstar of being reactionary and right wing.

- Pelé tried his hand at acting in several movies in the 1970s and '80s. The best-known film he appeared in, and the one where he had the largest role, was the 1981 sports-war film, *Escape to Victory*. Sylvester Stallone starred alongside Pelé in the film about Allied World War II POWs.

CHAPTER 5

JOSEPHINE BAKER: DIVA AND RESISTANCE FIGHTER

Most of the Black heroes and heroines in our book are known for excelling in one particular field in their lives, whether that be in the military, government, academics, or entertainment. A few of our Black heroes, though, had the talent, time, and patience to make an impact on the world in multiple areas.

Josephine Baker was one of these heroines.

Baker was born Freda Josephine McDonald in 1906 in St. Louis, Missouri. Life was difficult for young Freda, but she learned at an early age that she had a talent for dance, song, and generally entertaining people. She was exceptionally attractive and had a magnetism that drew people of all backgrounds to her, especially men.

Josephine eventually parlayed her natural assets into a lucrative career as a world-famous entertainer based primarily out of Paris, France. The path from poverty to fame alone, especially during the 1920s, would make Baker's story quite interesting and raise her to heroine status in many people's eyes, but that was only the beginning of her journey.

During World War II, Baker used her fame and looks to travel throughout German-occupied Europe and North Africa to spy on behalf of her adopted country of France.

Baker later became a figure in the American Civil Rights movement.

Through her combined work in entertainment, politics, and war, Josephine Baker became one of the most fascinating figures of the 20th century and a true international Black heroine. She continues to influence style and will forever be remembered for her interesting life.

The Mean Streets of St. Louis

Josephine was born to Carrie McDonald and an unknown father. She had a tough start life and things only got tougher. The United States was much different in 1906: segregation, both legal and otherwise, were the norm throughout the land; there were very few social safety nets; and basic services were far behind what they are today. If you were poor in the early 1900s, you often had to resort to extreme measures to survive.

For 13-year-old Josephine that meant getting married (yes, that was legal in 1919).

Josephine's marriage only lasted about a year, but she remarried in 1921 to Willie Baker, from whom she took her famous surname. Baker's second marriage only lasted until 1925, which meant that she was already divorced twice by the time she was 19.

For most women at that time being divorced once - never mind twice - by 19 would have been a socially-destroying stigma, but it didn't slow down Baker. She began dancing in vaudeville shows in St. Louis in the late 1910's and by 1921; Baker had made it to New York.

Josephine Baker didn't need either of her husbands for support. Baker didn't need any man, although she did like their company, marrying twice more after achieving international fame.

Baker was truly a talented dancer and an attractive woman, but as with all successful entertainers, she was helped by being in the right place at the right time. For Baker, that meant hitting her stride in the "Roaring Twenties."

International Fame and Resistance

America in the 1920s was an interesting time and place, full of many apparent contradictions. Prohibition was the law but speakeasies were common in the cities and it was still legal to possess booze. Segregation, legal and de facto, were also the law but live entertainment that featured Black musicians and dancers, but barred Black patrons, was also common.

Baker was able to break into the entertainment business in this environment, but it was in France where she became a worldwide phenomenon.

Anything and everything "exotic" was the rage in Western Europe, especially France, in the late 1910s and 1920s. Musical and dance revues featuring the sounds and sights of Asia and Africa were quite popular as Europe's vaudeville equivalent at the time, with such acts as Mata Hari becoming sell-out headlining acts. Baker quickly capitalized on this in 1925, performing a now-iconic dance wearing a skirt made of bananas and nothing but beads to cover her breasts.

The French people loved Josephine Baker.

To the French, and many other Europeans, she was exotic, but still somewhat familiar. Baker was African-American so she spoke English and was essentially Western in outlook. She also had a lighter-toned complexion, which appealed to Europeans.

By the 1930s, Baker had expanded her repertoire to include singing and acting, appearing in numerous films, and often appeared in her live acts topless. She was quite the trend-setter and like Mata Hari a few years prior, Baker traveled Europe and engaged in several romances with many influential men.

But when Germany conquered and occupied France in 1941, Baker's career seemed threatened. She didn't know if the Nazis would allow Blacks to keep performing, but apparently, they had more important things to think of - or they had contradictions of their own - because they allowed her to travel throughout German-occupied territory.

So Baker decided to follow in the footsteps of the infamous Mata Hari once more.

Throughout World War II, Baker observed what she saw and reported to the French Resistance and the Allies. She even cozied up to the enemy by hosting parties and gatherings and then reporting what she heard to the Allies. For her service with the French Resistance, Baker was awarded the Légion d'Honneur, which she proudly wore on several occasions throughout her life.

In the years after World War II, Baker continued to work in the entertainment industry but dedicated much of her time to the burgeoning Civil Rights movement in the United States. Baker was the only woman to speak at the historically important 1963 March on Washington in Washington, D.C, which was headlined by Martin Luther King Junior.

Baker continued to do performances until she died in 1975 at the age of 68 in Paris. Josephine Baker truly had several lives worth of adventures during her impactful life and has since inspired countless numbers to follow their dreams, wherever that may lead. For those reasons, Josephine Baker is one of the world's greatest Black heroines.

DID YOU KNOW?

- Baker adopted 12 children during her lifetime. The children were from a variety of races, nationalities, and religions, leading Baker to refer to the family as her "rainbow tribe."

- Several factors contributed to Baker never being as popular in the U.S. as in Europe. Her race was certainly a factor, but America's more conservative views generally prevented many of her performances from becoming mainstream. Also, her long absence from the United States didn't help.

- Baker often lived above her means, which led her to lose many of her properties later in her life.

- Baker performed in Cuba for dictator Fidel Castro in 1966. Baker was a French citizen and had been for quite some time, so the visit was perfectly legal.

- Due to her support of the Civil Rights movement and general left-wing political beliefs, Baker was occasionally accused of having communist sympathies in the 1950s and '60s.

CHAPTER 6

BOOKER T. WASHINGTON: BRINGING EDUCATION TO FORMER SLAVES

The institution of slavery was a problem in every country where it was practiced and where it still is practiced, for that matter. It created an unhealthy sense of dependency between different groups of people that was usually based on fear and degradation. When the Civil War ended slavery in the United States, the new status of freed Blacks seemed to create just as many problems for the country. There was lingering resentment by many Whites in the South, and most Blacks were suddenly thrust into a position that they had little understanding of, often leading to their exploitation.

Politicians from both major political parties at the time thought they had the answers.

The Republicans, who were basically liberals at the time, believed that White Southerners should be punished by placing newly freed Blacks in positions of power over them. Needless to say, this philosophy didn't do much to help racial reconciliation and often led to violent reactions. The Democrats favored a system whereby Blacks were kept in an inferior social position not much better than they were during slavery.

The Republicans and their ideas got the upper hand for the first ten years or so after the Civil War before the Democrats took power throughout the south, ushering in the system of segregation that lasted until the 1960s.

But what did Black Americans think about the situation?

Notable Black civil rights leader W.E.B. Dubois believed that Blacks should push for full equality under the law by challenging segregation laws and voting restrictions in the courts. Later, the ideas of Dubois were picked up by civil rights leaders such as Martin Luther King Junior, but they weren't the only strain of thought at the time among African-Americans.

Some Black leaders believed that a more conservative, pragmatic approach should be taken. These leaders argued that Black Americans needed to be educated in trades and business before they could think about taking any sort of political power. They also argued that it was important to work with the White power structure, not against it.

By far the most prominent leader of this philosophy was Booker Taliaferro Washington, better known as Booker T. Washington.

Washington was born a slave but died one of the most influential Americans of his time and a true Black hero. He may not have invented the idea of historically Black colleges and universities (HBCUs), but his work at the Hampton Institute in Virginia in the late 1870s and his founding of the famous Tuskegee Institute in Alabama in 1881 helped spread the idea. Due to Washington's efforts, thousands of Black Americans were able to attain college educations in the era of segregation and countless more were able to become self-sufficient by starting businesses.

Booker T. Washington's image has undergone several reassessments since he died in 1915, but today most scholars agree that he was a true Black hero.

Up from Slavery

Booker T. Washington was born in 1856 in rural Virginia as a slave to a woman named Jane and an unknown White man. He lived through the Civil War as a child and eventually migrated with his family to the new state of West Virginia. He took the surname from his mother's husband's first name and his middle name from his former owner.

Washington was a man who never harbored grudges and didn't believe in living in the past.

Life in Malden, West Virginia wasn't easy for Booker and his family. They were definitely on the bottom rung of the socio-economic ladder, often finding themselves competing with European immigrants and poor local Whites for the most menial of jobs. From a young age, Booker had to work because his stepfather was often unable to provide for the family. Needless to say, Booker's stepfather was never a good role model, but the young man never let that get him down. Booker always had a good disposition and most importantly, he was always willing to learn new things, whether it be on the many jobs he held or how to read and write.

The bright young Washington taught himself the basics of literacy and with the help of some wealthy benefactors, he was introduced to classic literature and more advanced grammar.

He also learned about the Hampton Institute.

The Hampton Institute, now known as Hampton University, was founded in 1868 as one of the nation's first HBCUs. Its early focus was on teaching freedmen (former slaves) vocational and business skills that they could use to be self-sufficient. When Washington finally arrived there in 1872, he was impressed with the curriculum and quickly became one of the school's top students.

Washington worked as a janitor to pay for his tuition but soon became a tutor and after graduating, a professor. At that point, Washington could've sat back, relaxed, and lived a comfortable life in Hampton, Virginia. He was a respected member of Hampton's Black *and* White communities, had a nice job, and would later marry. And who could've blamed him if that was his choice? After all, he'd lived such a tough life, he deserved to have it good, right?

Well, Washington was an extremely ambitious and visionary man, so when prominent members of the Black community asked him to start a new HBCU in Tuskegee, Alabama in 1881, he jumped at the offer.

Educating His People

The original school was on the grounds of a former church, but Washington expanded the campus a year later by 100 acres. With the help of the students, Washington built new meeting halls and dormitories that provided the core for what would later become Tuskegee University.

And as Tuskegee slowly but surely became a success, Washington used his charisma and superb oratorical skills to convince wealthy Whites to contribute to Tuskegee and other HBCUs. By the time Washington died in 1915 at the early age of 59, he had spoken at the 1895 World's Fair in Atlanta, delivered speeches in several states and in Europe, and even dined with President Theodore Roosevelt in the White House in 1901. He was the first African-American to officially dine in the White House.

As the Civil Rights movement became more pronounced in the 1960s and peaceful protests gave way to the often violent radicalism of the Black Panthers and other similar groups, many Black leaders and academics took a negative view of Washington, seeing him as an "appeaser." But by the 1990s, views of Washington and his mission had become more pragmatic and sympathetic.

Today, most scholars and civil rights activists see Booker T. Washington as one of the most influential African-American figures in the early 20th century and a true Black hero for his efforts to bring education to his people.

DID YOU KNOW?

- Washington was married three times and had three children, one with his first wife and two with his second wife. Washington's first two wives preceded him in death.

- Besides being an excellent speaker, teacher, and administrator, Washington was also a writer. He wrote five books, the most famous of which was *Up from Slavery*, published in 1901. As the title indicates, the book chronicles his journey from slavery to freedom and relates his philosophies on education as well as touching on race and politics.

- There are currently 14 American high schools named after Booker T. Washington.

- The place where Washington was born near Hardy, Virginia was commemorated as the Booker T. Washington National Monument 1956. A statue of Washington marks the location.

- After dying of complications from high blood pressure, Washington was buried on the grounds of the Tuskegee Institute.

CHAPTER 7

BOB MARLEY: INSPIRING A NEW GENERATION

Many of the Black heroes in this book became so by affecting legislation in their respective countries through their positions as government leaders or via activism. We saw how Haile Selassie led his country and later we'll see how activists such as Martin Luther King Junior influenced change through programs of protest. We'll also see how South African leader

Nelson Mandela affected change by working *against* the government, then with it, and finally *within* it as a leader.

We've also seen how some men and women became notable Black heroes by inspiring others.

Booker T. Washington inspired former slaves to educate themselves, Pelé inspired people around the world to come together in their love of sport, and Josephine Baker inspired others to be themselves but also to stand up for their beliefs.

Add Jamaican reggae musician Bob Marley to this list of inspiring Black heroes.

To those not very familiar with Bob Marley, dreadlocks and marijuana smoke immediately come to mind, but there was so much more to the reggae musician from central Jamaica.

Bob Marley was one of the major musicians who helped to popularize reggae, helping it go mainstream. By doing so, Marley inspired countless musicians in the Caribbean, North America, and Europe to emulate his musical style, look, and beliefs. Marley was also instrumental in introducing thousands, if not millions, of White people to reggae and ska music.

Due to his musical talents and overall cool look and style, Bob Marley became not only a 20th-century musical icon, but also an inspirational Black hero to millions across the globe.

Jamaica Isn't Always Paradise

Just as many people have an image of Bob Marley as little more than a pot-smoking musician, many also have a false notion of Jamaica as a peaceful paradise. Sure, Jamaica has some beautiful weather and beaches, but once you get beyond the popular resorts, which are usually secure compounds, you'll find that it is a poor country with plenty of crime.

This was the world Robert Nesta Marley was born into in 1945.

Bob was born in the central highlands region of Jamaica to a White Jamaican businessman father, Norval Marley, and a Black Jamaican mother, Cedella. Marley's family was financially secure and middle class, by Jamaican standards, for the first few years of his life, but tragedy struck in 1955 when his father died of a heart attack.

As bad as this turn of events was for the young Marley, tragedy and adversity are what seems to drive all great men and women in world history, helping to make them heroes and heroines. Adversity is also good for the tortured soul of musicians, often giving them plenty of material and inspiration for their work. But Marley's father's death also proved to be somewhat of a fortuitous event for his later musical career as well.

Roots Reggae

Marley's mother remarried and moved her family to the Trenchtown neighborhood of the capital city of Kingston. By the 1960s, Trenchtown was the most happening and culturally relevant spot in Jamaica. It was where many Jamaican actors lived, but more importantly for Marley, it was also the heart of Kingston's vibrant music scene.

The sounds of American Jazz and blues along with Caribbean calypso and Jamaican ska constantly wafted from the neighborhood's bars and homes.

Having a good voice and ear or music, Bob formed an a cappella group with Bunny Wailer, Peter Tosh, and others that would comprise the core of his famous band, The Wailers. Eventually, Marley learned how to play the guitar and the other members picked up the saxophone, trumpet, trombone, and drums, to become one of the best-known Jamaican ska bands of the 1960s.

The Bob Marley and the Wailers of the early to mid-1960s had a very different style to what Marley is known for now.

Marley and the Wailers adopted a clean, "Rudeboy" look, wearing suits and ties with short haircuts. And although the ska style certainly influenced reggae, the Wailers' ska albums were much more upbeat with lyrics that focused on women, parties, and just having a good time.

Despite his fame in Jamaica, and the United Kingdom to a certain extent, Marley was a restless soul who was always looking to challenge himself by acquiring new knowledge and experiencing new things. So in 1966, he moved to the United States, married, and worked for a short time at a factory in Wilmington, Delaware.

Bob wasn't giving up music; this was all just a part of his long journey to find himself. In 1968, he did, after he converted to Rastafarianism.

Remember Haile Selassie and Rastafarianism from the first chapter? Well, Marley was impressed with Selassie's visit, so he began to read up on and meet with Jamaican Rastafarians, eventually converting to the religion.

By 1969, Marley brought the Wailers into Rastafarianism and helped give them a new, more mellow musical style.

The horns that were such a prominent part of ska were downplayed in reggae in favor of organs, but more importantly, the beat was slowed down quite a bit. Also gone were the party lyrics, which were replaced with ones that focused on Pan-Africanism and all elements of Rastafarianism, which included marijuana use.

Marley also grew his hair into dreadlocks to emphasize a more natural look and the Wailers traded in their suits and ties for jeans and t-shirts.

Bob Marley may not have invented reggae, but he was one of the earliest reggae artists. He was also one of the earliest artists to emphasize the "roots" sub-genre of reggae, which emphasizes Afrocentrism, although Marley's style was far less militant and appealed to a larger audience, including millions of White young people.

Marley recorded 13 studio albums, two live albums, and toured throughout the world in his short but very influential career. There is little doubt that Marley would have recorded many more albums, and still would be recording, if he hadn't died at the young age of 36 from skin cancer in 1981.

Despite being gone for nearly 40 years, Bob Marley continues to inspire young people around the globe, of all races, which makes him truly an inspirational Black hero.

DID YOU KNOW?

- Music was a family affair in the Marley home. His wife Rita was a singer in the Wailers and many of Bob's 11 children (he had four with Rita) are professional musicians. Son Ziggy has had the most success in the music business.

- Marley's pan-Africanist beliefs were heavily influenced by early 20th-century Jamaican activist Marcus Garvey. Many of these ideas can be heard throughout Marley's music, such as in the song "Buffalo Soldier," which related the history of Black American frontier soldiers in the late 1800s.

- Marley was connected to two of our other Black heroes in this book. As a follower of Rastafarianism, Marley believed that Haile Selassie was the Messiah. Marley was also a lifelong fan of Brazilian football club Santos and Pelé.

- Marley and his wife survived an assassination attempt at their home in Jamaica in 1976. The couple and a friend were shot by an unknown, would-be assassin. This is believed to have been connected to the turbulent political situation at the time in the country.

- Marley died of a rare form of skin cancer known as acral lentiginous melanoma. It is a rapidly spreading disease that is often missed in exams because it often starts under the feet, or in Marley's case, under one of his toenails. Although skin cancer, in general, more commonly affects people of northern European descent, acral lentiginous melanoma is the primary type of skin cancer people with darker complexions contract.

CHAPTER 8

KWAME NKRUMAH: AFRICAN INDEPENDENCE HERO

History has shown that not everything or everyone is cut and dry, black and white, including heroes and heroines. The world can be a pretty complex place, especially in geopolitics, where friends one minute can be enemies the next. Our next Black hero is one such man who went from being a true African hero one minute to an absolute dictator and zero the next.

Kwame Nkrumah rode the wave of nationalist and anti-colonial feelings in West Africa during the 1950s to become the premier leader of the African independence movement. Like Bob Marley, Nkrumah advocated a pan-Africanist philosophy that sought to help Black people and nations in Africa, the Caribbean, and the Americas.

Eventually, Nkrumah's anti-colonial efforts led to the creation of the modern nation-state of Ghana in 1957 with him as the head of state as its first prime minister.

Nkrumah was so popular with the Ghanaian people that, in 1960, they approved a new constitution that made their leader the president. Apparently, Nkrumah let the power, prestige, and popularity go to his head because, in 1964, he made himself dictator for life.

Needless to say, his popularity quickly waned and he was deposed and exiled in 1964, never to return to his homeland.

For decades, Nkrumah was relegated to being classified as a standard dictator along with a variety of others, right wing and left wing, from around the world. But in recent years, his image and rule have been reassessed, leading many to see him as a legitimate Black hero.

Sure, he was a dictator, they argue, but he was far from brutal and genuinely understood the often precarious political position that African rulers at the time faced. Many see his efforts to bring about African unity and peace in the region as a positive legacy and point to modern Ghana's economic and social stability as the fruits of what Nkrumah attempted to achieve in the 1950s and '60s.

Traveling the World

Kwame Nkrumah was born in 1909 to a poor family in the then-British colony of the Gold Coast, today Ghana. Despite lacking in means, young Nkrumah was given plenty of latitude by his family to pursue academic interests and was accepted into some of the colony's best Catholic schools. It was while in Catholic school that Nkrumah first became interested in history, economics, and politics, with a special interest in the history of the African diaspora.

Nkrumah's teachers knew that he had the potential to do something great with his life, so they urged him to apply to a school in Europe or the United States. Nkrumah wanted to attend school at the London School of Economics but was rejected.

The rejection hit him hard, but one of his teachers suggested he apply to Lincoln University, a HBCU outside Philadelphia, Pennsylvania.

Nkrumah was accepted and began his schooling there in 1935.

The experience proved to be important in many ways for Nkrumah. He began going by the more Western-sounding name "Francis" while in America, in an attempt to fit in better with his peers. By all accounts, he did fit in well with his American peers, but he preferred to hang out with Caribbean and African ex-pats in Philadelphia and New York.

When he wasn't hanging out with ex-pats and organizing study sessions and discussions groups with them, he was studying theology and politics, especially socialist philosophers. Nkrumah graduated at the head of his class at Lincoln in 1942, earning a BA in theology and then a MA in theology at the prestigious Penn the next year.

Nkurmah seemed well on his way to doing something great with his life by the time World War II ended.

Francis finally got his chance to go to school in London in 1945, but he never earned another degree. He was described as a dreamer who wanted results quickly and wasn't patient enough to let the scientific process happen.

Undeterred, Nkurmah returned home in 1946 with new ideas and a vision for the future of his people and country. He was going to change things one way or another.

Onward to Independence

Almost as soon as Nkrumah arrived back at the Gold Coast, he began organizing his people into an independence movement. He first helped form the United Gold Coast Convention, which later became the Convention People's Party. By the early 1950s, it was clear to the British that the Gold Coast was going to become independent, so it was just a matter of putting "their guys" into power.

Nkrumah was not one of the Brits' guys.

He was seen as too much of a leftist who could cozy up with the Soviet Union. Still, there was little the British could do as Nkrumah led the colony of the Gold Coast to become the independent nation of Ghana on March 6, 1957. Ghana was the first of Britain's sub-Saharan colonies to achieve self-rule and did so peacefully and in an orderly manner.

The first few years of Nkrumah's rule went exceptionally well. He all but eliminated many of the nation's tribal rivalries, raised the country's GDP through cocoa exports, and along with Haile Selassie, played a leading role in the formation of the Organization of African Unity.

But as was the case in Africa, and still is, governments are only a step away from being overthrown.

Nkrumah walked a tight rope between the Western and communist worlds. He developed close relations with the Soviet Union, communist Cuba, and other communist states, which did not sit well with the US, UK, and other Western powers. Once he assumed total power over Ghana in 1964, it was just a matter of time before people in his own government would make a move against him.

The moment came when Nkrumah was visiting the communist states of North Vietnam and China in February 1966. The Ghana military assumed power and declared Nkrumah an enemy of the state and immediately reversed his geopolitical philosophy by realigning Ghana with the West.

Nkrumah lived the rest of his life in exile in the African nation of Guinea. He died on April 27, 1972, of prostate cancer while visiting the communist state of Romania.

After his death, Nkrumah was celebrated in the Eastern Bloc as an anti-colonial freedom fighter and patriot. Today, his reputation has been largely rehabilitated in Ghana as they view him as the father of the country. Throughout the world, he is seen as a pan-African Black hero.

DID YOU KNOW?

- Ghana is a multi-tribal, multi-ethnic nation. Nkrumah was a member of the Akan people, which are the largest single group in the country, but just under 50% of the population.

- Nkrumah was named Kwame following West African naming traditions. All males born on a Saturday were named Kwame.

- Nkrumah married an Egyptian woman named Fathia in 1957, the same year he became prime minister. The couple had four children.

- Although Nkrumah was not a brutal dictator, he did practice authoritarian rule and employed many tactics typical dictators use, such as building a cult of personality. Nkrumah had his image put on stamps, money, posters, and billboards throughout Ghana during his rule.

- The British Broadcasting Company World Service declared Nkrumah the "African Man of the Millennium" in 2000 as a "hero of independence."

CHAPTER 9

TAHARQA: ANCIENT BLACK WARRIOR AND KING

Ancient Egypt is one of the best known of all ancient societies today, and for good reason: along with Mesopotamia, Egypt was the first true civilization to form (around 3,100 BCE); its pyramids and temples have withstood the test of time; and its abundant corpus of literature that has survived has allowed modern scholars to know much about the ancient world. Of course, you probably know that ancient Egyptian civilization began on the banks of the Nile River and grew along the river from where the Delta meets the Mediterranean Sea in the north to where it ends at Aswan in the south.

But south of ancient Egypt, there was an ancient Black society that at times rivaled the Egyptians.

South of modern Aswan is what is known as the first cataract. A cataract is a rocky part of a river that is unnavigable, and in ancient times, it marked the effective border between Egypt and Nubia, or "Kush" as the Egyptians called it. Essentially, ancient Nubia/Kush is congruent with modern Sudan.

The ancient Nubian people developed a culture that was deeply influenced by Egypt, worshipping many of the same gods and even building pyramids for their deceased kings.

But Nubian culture also had distinct, sub-Saharan African elements.

Many of the buildings in early Nubian history were circular, as in other parts of Africa, and they continued to worship many gods of their own. The Nubian pyramids were also notably different from their Egyptian counterparts, having 60° to 73° sides, giving them a notably slender look.

Nubia was generally overshadowed by Egypt and was often ruled and colonized by the Egyptians, although whenever Egypt experienced periods of turmoil and decline, powerful Nubian kingdoms formed. When Egypt entered a period of decline known as the Third Intermediate around 1000 BCE, Nubia entered into its greatest period in history.

In 728 BCE, the Nubian King Piye led an army into Egypt, vanquishing Libyan chieftains who had divided the country between themselves, and ushering in more than 150 years of Nubian rule that Egyptologists refer to as the Twenty-Fifth Dynasty.

The Nubians ruled Egypt as legitimate pharaohs by building monuments and conducting diplomacy and warfare in the name of the Egyptian gods.

Among these Nubian kings, perhaps the most interesting was a guy named Taharqa, or Taharqo.

The Warrior Prince

Another factor that separated the Nubians from the Egyptians was how the former chose their kings. Generally speaking, the Egyptians followed the standard method whereby the oldest son would become king, but the Nubians appear to have often passed the kingship between brothers and/or cousins before passing it to the younger generation.

After Piye' rule, the throne passed to Shabaqa (ruled 716-702 BCE) and then probably Shebitqu (reigned 702-690 BCE).

Taharqa was most likely the son of Piye, so he had to wait for his uncles to pass the torch before he could rule. By all accounts, Taharqa appears to have been a patient young man, which contributed to his success when he finally achieved the mantle of power.

Taharqa was born around· the time his father died, so he learned about warfare and kingship from his family and royal advisors. It was a dangerous part of the world and the geopolitical situation was ever-changing. The mighty Assyrian Empire was engulfing kingdom after kingdom and had just conquered the Kingdom of Israel when the Kingdom of Judah approached the Nubians for aid sometime either in or just before 701 BCE.

According to royal inscriptions from the Nubian city of Kawa, Shebitqu called Taharqa (from the Nubian capital city of Napata to the Egyptian capital of Memphis in 701 BCE) to lead a most important mission—he would lead a combined Egyptian-Nubian army north to support Hezekiah of Judah against King Sennacherib (ruled 704-681 BCE) of Assyria.

The armies met on a plain near the city of Eltekh.

The epic battle was chronicled in the Old Testament book of 2 Kings 19:9-37 and in numerous Assyrian texts. In the Bible, Taharqa is called "Tirhakah King of Ethiopia," which is not completely inaccurate. Since Taharqa did later become king and since the Bible was *written* after the events, it was understandable that he was referred to as a king. And as for the term "Ethiopia," Nubia was often referred to as such by the Greeks, Romans, and Hebrews.

The Battle of Eltekh was technically a draw, although the Assyrian temporarily retreated, only to conquer the region under a later king. Taharqa was possibly wounded in battle, which only seemed to enhance his reputation at the royal court and among the people.

The Battle of Eltekh ensured that Taharqa would become known as one of Nubia's greatest kings.

Ruling Nubia and Egypt

The Kawa texts state that Taharqa led the expedition to Judah at the age of 20, which means that when he finally ascended the dual Egyptian-Nubian throne, he was only about 25. That is pretty incredible when you think about it!

Today, most 25-year-olds are just starting their adult lives, beginning their careers and starting families. At that age, Taharqa was handed the incredibly daunting responsibility of ruling a vast empire and having to contend with the ever-present threats from the bellicose Assyrians!

By all accounts, Taharqa did just fine.

The most notable Egyptian rulers were known for many feats, but most important was their ability to build new monuments and to refurbish and add to existing structures. In this regard, Taharqa was on par with most Egyptian kings and outdid his Nubian predecessors.

Taharqa dedicated most of his building activities to the area around the southern Egyptian city of Thebes, adding a major gateway, called a "pylon," to the Temple of Karnak. The King also added several other smaller monuments in the region. Thebes was important to Taharqa due to its proximity to Nubia and because it was the "home" of the god Amun, who was also worshipped extensively by the Nubians.

But helping the Judeans against the Assyrians brought the wrath of the latter against Egypt and Nubia.

As Taharqa was building monuments in Egypt, the Assyrian King Esarhaddon (reigned 680-669 BCE) was preparing a major punitive expedition against Taharqa. Taharqa was able to defeat the first Assyrian attack in 674 BCE, but it only seemed to anger the Assyrians, who returned with a force large enough to conquer northern Egypt later that year.

Taharqa's family was deported to Assyria and he was left with a major life-changing decision to make. Should he retreat to Napata where he would more than likely be safe from the Assyrians, or counterattack? Ever the consummate warrior, Taharqa chose to attack.

The Egyptian-Nubian counterattack was quickly defeated and followed up by the Assyrian King Assurbanipal (ruled 680-631 BCE) sacking Thebes and establishing a puppet government in 669 or 668 BCE.

All seemed lost, but Taharqa still had one last card to play. He instigated a rebellion among the Assyrian puppet governors, but it was quickly suppressed and Taharqa was killed, ending the period of Nubian dominance in Egypt.

Although Taharqa's kingdom ultimately collapsed, he demonstrated incredible martial skills, political foresight, and tenacity throughout his short but impactful life. Taharqa understood that, for his kingdom to survive, it needed to be a major player in the "game of thrones" that was taking place in the ancient Near East at the time. He also knew that the

Assyrians were a people who weren't open to compromise, so he had to fight them until the bitter end. For these reasons, Taharqa is often remembered as one of the first Black military heroes in world history.

DID YOU KNOW?

- Nubian royal succession has been a confusing and controversial topic among many Egyptologists for years. There was once a consensus that Shebitqu was Taharqa's successor, but today there are many scholars who believe it was Shabaqa.

- If you ever have the chance of visiting the Karnak Temple in modern-day Luxor, Egypt, the first pylon you see is the one built by Taharqa.

- Like most rulers in the ancient Near East and Egypt, Taharqa had several wives and concubines, although only one "chief queen": Takahatenamum. She was probably Taharqa's sister.

- There are several extant statues of Taharqa in museums throughout the world. A black granite head of the king is currently housed in the Nubia Museum in Aswan, Egypt and a black granite colossal statue of Taharqa is the centerpiece of the National Museum of Sudan in Khartoum, Sudan.

- Taharqa was buried under a pyramid in the royal necropolis near Nuri, Sudan.

CHAPTER 10

ELLA FITZGERALD: THE QUEEN OF JAZZ

There are hundreds of truly excellent musicians who've produced and recorded phenomenal music over the last several decades, a handful that've influenced the course of a musical style, and an even smaller group who've defined several genres and even an era.

Ella Fitzgerald is among that rare era-defining group.

Often called the "Queen of Jazz" for her recording of countless jazz and blues hits during the 1930s, Fitzgerald proved to the world that she could chart hits in several genres, including swing, pop, and early rock n roll. Fitzgerald began recording her music in the late 1930's and by the time she made her last recording in 1991, she had recorded hundreds of singles, full albums, live albums, and dozens of chart-topping hits. She had four #1 hits on the US charts and three #1 hits on the US R&B charts.

And things were never easy for Fitzgerald.

Although she arrived in this world with a strong voice and musical talents, she was also born into a life of poverty that seemed hopeless at times. After working her way out of poverty, she rose to fame and was loved by Black *and* White fans at a time when there was limited interaction between the races in America.

Fitzgerald eventually brought her unique style and diverse musical talents to the world, selling out shows on multiple continents. During her lifetime, Fitzgerald was recognized for her musical talent, hard work, dignity, and class through numerous awards. For many young musicians, Ella Fitzgerald was, and remains, a Black heroine of the music world.

From Virginia to Harlem

As with many of the heroes and heroines in this book, Ella Fitzgerald's early life was one of poverty, disappointments, and struggle. She was born Ella Jane Fitzgerald in 1917 to an unmarried couple in Newport News, Virginia, which was certainly more than enough to raise a few eyebrows at the time, even in the poorest of neighborhoods. Ella's father and mother broke up before she was six, and in 1923, she moved with her mother and her new boyfriend to Yonkers, New York.

It was a very unstable way to start a life.

Although Ella showed musical promise at a very early age, her mother did little to nurture those interests or abilities, and then tragedy struck.

When Ella was just 15, her mother died in a car accident. The tragedy sent the teen reeling and onto the mean streets of Harlem, where she survived by living on the margins of society and the law.

Ella eventually took to earning money by singing on the corners of streets in Harlem and eventually was noticed for her talent. People would tell her to try out for the amateur night at the famous Apollo Theater, but Ella knew she couldn't just go in without a good act. The crowd at the Apollo was known for being harsh, but when the 17-year-old Fitzgerald took the stage, they couldn't help but fall in love with the girl's strong voice.

Fitzgerald won the crowd at the Apollo and set herself up for a long, successful career in the music business.

It Don't Mean a Thing (If It Ain't Got That Swing)

Fitzgerald's rise to fame was meteoric, to say the least. By the late 1930's, she was recording hits with some of the biggest names in the big band scene, including Dizzy Gillespie and the Benny Goodman Orchestra. Things were going well for Ella, but before long, as is always the case with popular music, tastes and styles began to change. The big band era was over by the late 1940s and in its place was the "bebop" style, which later gave way to rhythm and blues and rock n roll.

So Fitzgerald decided to change with the times as well.

If there's one thing that characterizes Ella Fitzgerald's long and successful career, it was her ability to adapt to constantly evolving musical styles. Fitzgerald was always at the forefront of new genres, but through it all, she always produced music that appealed to wide audiences and was often very catchy. As the 1967 version of the song "It Don't Mean a Thing" states, "If It Ain't Got That Swing"…

By the 1960s, Ella Fitzgerald had effectively crossed the racial barrier in the United States - and the world, for that matter. Yes, there were still places where she wasn't allowed and she was even once barred from a flight to Australia in the 1950s, but by the 1960s, Americans of all races knew and loved her music and recognized her as the "Queen of Jazz."

America's top crooners lined up to work with Fitzgerald in the 1960s and '70s, including Dean Martin, Nat King Cole, and old Blue Eyes, Frank Sinatra. And later in life, she was recognized for her lifetime of achievements when she performed at the White House for President Ronald Reagan and was awarded the Presidential Medal of Freedom by President George H.W. Bush in 1992.

When it comes to music, many would say that Ella Fitzgerald was more than just the Queen of Jazz—she was the First Lady of American Music.

DID YOU KNOW?

- Fitzgerald first played with older, established bands before taking over Chic Webb's orchestra in 1939 and renaming it Ella and Her Famous Orchestra.

- Ella was married twice. She and second husband, Ray Brown, adopted a son, Ray Brown Junior.

- Fitzgerald lived in New York City during the early years of her fame but eventually moved to Beverly Hills.

- Fitzgerald was known for having somewhat of an introverted personality and was a bit of a loner when not on stage, which surprised many people because she was so lively during her shows.

- Ella Fitzgerald died on June 15, 1996, from complications of diabetes at the age of 79. She was buried in her adopted home town of Beverly Hills, California.

CHAPTER 11

MARTIN LUTHER KING JUNIOR: *THE* CIVIL RIGHTS ICON

No book about the world's most prominent Black heroes and heroines would be complete without a chapter on Martin Luther King Junior, the civil rights icon of the United States. Long after King was assassinated in 1968, his words, ideas, and deeds carried on in the United States through legislation that was passed in his name. Throughout the world, his method of nonviolent resistance has been emulated by a diverse array of political movements.

Although many men and women took part in the American Civil Rights Movement of the 1950's and '60s, helping to make it a success, in many ways, King embodied the movement and is the first person who comes to most people's minds when they're asked about the subject.

Martin Luther King Junior faced many battles throughout his life. He fought segregation and discrimination in his personal life, faced challenges to his leadership within the Civil Rights Movement, and was opposed by militant segregationists throughout the United States (King faced more violent reactions to his marches and appearances in Chicago than anywhere).

In the end, Martin Luther King Junior died for his beliefs, but in the process, he was made a martyr. Today, he has his own Federal holiday, a national monument in Washington, D.C. (alongside those of many presidents), and is viewed as a hero by millions of people of all backgrounds. For those reasons, Martin Luther King Junior is often considered to be not only the premier civil rights hero but also first among all Black heroes.

Growing up with "Jim Crow"

You may not know this, but Martin Luther King Junior was born *Michael* King Junior on January 15, 1929 in Atlanta, Georgia. So what's up with the name? Well, King Senior was a minister at the world-famous Ebenezer Baptist Church in Atlanta. Of course, Ebenezer is famous now because it's known as the place where Martin Luther King Junior got his start, but it was well-known even in the 1930s as a center of African-American culture and theology in the American south.

Due to the church's reputation, King Senior was invited to visit several churches and dignitaries in Europe and the Middle East in 1934. After seeing some incredible sights and meeting some important people, King Senior was profoundly impacted when he visited Germany and experienced the places where the 16th Protestant reformer, Martin Luther, lived and studied. After returning to the states, he decided to change his and his son's first and middle name to honor Luther.

Although Junior grew up in a comfortable middle-class life in Atlanta, it was the era of the "Jim Crow" laws, where Blacks were legally segregated in public spaces and outright prohibited from some altogether.

King attended Booker T. Washington High School in inner-city Atlanta, where he showed great academic progress, even skipping a grade.

But where King showed the most promise was in his oratorical skills. He was especially gifted in delivering Bible verses and impressed his teachers and classmates in class presentations and debates. Most thought that King would be a successful minister like his father; few believed that he would lead a movement that would forever change the character of the United States of America.

Martin graduated from high school early and enrolled in Atlanta's Morehouse College, one of the oldest and most prestigious HBCUs in America.

Once he entered college, King was faced with one of the first major challenges of his life.

Perhaps he was too immature to handle the rigors of college life, and all the adult responsibilities that come with it, because he struggled through his first couple of years. He ended up graduating in 1948 with average marks, but it was enough to get him into divinity school at Crozer Theological Seminary in Pennsylvania. He may not have been the top student in any of his classes, but he was among the most ambitious. He earned a divinity degree in 1951, which landed him a spot at Boston University, where he obtained a Ph.D. in theology in 1954.

At that point, King could have rested on his laurels and pursued a comfortable life as a preacher. He had offers to preach at several churches around the country and to teach theology in numerous schools, but he chose to move back to the South.

Martin Luther King Junior was interested in more than comfort and money.

A Higher Calling

Months after earning his Ph.D., King took a position as pastor at the Dexter Avenue Baptist Church in Montgomery, Alabama. This was a familiar environment to the southern born and raised King, but he had bigger ideas in mind when he took the position.

He was going to challenge legalized segregation in the heart of the South.

King had grown up with segregation in Georgia, but it wasn't quite the same as in Alabama and Mississippi. Those two states were certainly the heart of Dixie and the "Deep South," and when the *Brown v. Board of Education of Topeka* came down in May 1954, they became ground zero in the war to end segregation.

King made the conscious choice to be at the center of that battle, no matter what it may cost.

It didn't take King long to enter the fray of the civil rights war. On December 1, 1955, civil rights activist Rosa Parks decided not to give up her seat on a Montgomery, Alabama public bus for a White rider. King and other civil rights activists descended on Montgomery to enact the "Montgomery Bus Boycott," which was intended to desegregate the city's public bus system.

King quickly learned that this truly was a war in Alabama, as he survived an assassination attempt and was briefly jailed for civil disobedience. Eventually, though, the United States

Supreme Court overturned the segregation policy of the Montgomery public transit system. At the time, it seemed like a minor victory, but it was really the beginning of a wave of pro-Civil Rights legislation.

And Martin Luther King Junior turned out to be the national public face of the Civil Rights Movement.

King became the head of the Southern Christian Leadership Conference (SCLC), which was the vanguard of the Civil Rights Movement in the 1960s. As the leader of the organization and the de facto leader of the movement, King met with presidents and was a vital organizer and speaker at many notable civil rights demonstrations and events.

The most notable speech King gave was his "I Have a Dream" speech in front of an estimated 300,000 people on August 28, 1963, at the March on Washington for Jobs and Freedom.

The speech, combined with his efforts and collaborations with other activists, led to some of the most sweeping civil rights legislation in American history. In 1964, Congress passed, and President Lyndon Johnson signed, the Civil Rights Act of 1964, outlawing racial segregation and discrimination. A year later, the Voting Rights Act of 1965 was passed, allowing millions of Blacks in the South to vote for the first time in their lives.

No man did more to change racial laws and policies in the United States than Martin Luther King Junior, which is probably what ultimately led to his assassination in Memphis, Tennessee on April 4, 1968.

During his life, King became an icon and hero, and in death he became a martyr. Because of the life he lived and the changes he affected, many people consider Martin Luther King Junior first and foremost among all Black heroes.

DID YOU KNOW?

- King was shot and killed as he stood on the balcony of his room at the Lorraine Motel, just south of downtown Memphis. The site where he was assassinated is today part of the National Civil Rights Museum.

- The fatal shot was fired from a room in a boarding house next to the motel. The police found the rifle in the boarding house and traced fingerprints on it to career criminal James Earl Ray (1928-1998). Ray was captured with a false Canadian passport two months later in the United Kingdom. Due to Ray not having any known connections to far right-wing groups or ideologies, and the fact that he seemed so well supported and supplied for a routine criminal, many believe the assassination was part of a wider conspiracy. Ray confessed and was sentenced to life in prison, but later recanted the confession.

- King married his wife Coretta in 1953. They had four children.

- Similar to Booker T. Washington, more radical elements sometimes saw King as an "appeaser," although his reputation has generally been more favorable than that.

- The Martin Luther King Junior memorial covers four acres of ground near the National Mall, with its centerpiece being the statue of King called the *Stone of* Hope. The statue was carved by Chinese sculptor Lei Yixin, and the entire memorial was opened to the public on August 22, 2011.

CHAPTER 12

MANSA MUSA: THE WEALTHIEST MAN IN THE WORLD

Europeans once referred to Africa, particularly sub-Saharan Africa, as the "Dark Continent," not because its people were Black, but because so much of it remained a mystery to them. It wasn't until the mid to late 1800s that European explorers such as David Livingstone and Henry Stanley made forays deep into the African interior, documenting and mapping what they found for a European audience.

And what they found was plenty of wealth.

There were large gold deposits, diamonds, and other valuable minerals throughout sub-Saharan Africa, leading to the colonial competition between Britain, France, Belgium, and Germany that left almost every part of the continent ruled by one of the European powers.

But none of this was news to the people who had lived in sub-Saharan Africa for centuries. To them it wasn't a "Dark Continent" and little about it was mysterious. The gold and diamond deposits of sub-Saharan Africa were well-known to the various tribes and kingdoms of the continent, and to many, they seemed virtually worthless. After all, most pre-colonial African economic systems were based on barter, which is itself based on practical necessity; and what practical value do gold or diamonds have?

Of course, gold and diamonds have value if you trade them to people who value them.

Some African peoples, such as the Nubians, are known to have traded gold to outsiders in ancient times, but no African ruler stockpiled the precious metal more than King Mansa Musa I (ruled c. 1312-1337) of the Mali Empire. Although Mansa Musa's kingdom's economy was barter-based, and therefore had no practical need for gold, he was active in foreign affairs, developing contacts with Muslim rulers in North Africa and the Middle East. The one thing Mali had at the time was plenty of gold, so whenever Mansa Musa met foreign dignitaries or traveled to the Middle East, he made sure to bring plenty of gold and give most of it away.

Mansa Musa's displays of wealth may have been ostentatious, but he also gave plenty to the poor and funded the construction of mosques and schools throughout Africa. The King's many deeds eventually earned him a reputation as the "wealthiest man in the world" and a true hero to the poor and downtrodden. Still, due to a lack of proper documentation, Mansa Musa is probably the least understood hero in our book.

A Powerful African Kingdom

As Europeans were building cathedrals and castles and the Chinese were building the Great Wall in the Middle Ages, sophisticated African kingdoms were also beginning to develop. The first major medieval African kingdom to develop was Ghana, but it was conquered by Mali. It's important to know that some modern African nation-states have taken their names from medieval kingdoms, although they don't necessarily correspond exactly with their fore bearer's names geographically. The medieval kingdom of Mali roughly consisted of the land of modern Mali and the modern country of Mauritania in west-central Africa.

Most of what modern scholars know about Mali comes from medieval Arab scholars and historians since no form of writing had developed yet in that part of the world. The Arab writers noted that although the rulers of Mali were pious Muslims, they didn't force the religion on their subject and had lifestyles that were often quite different from what was the norm for Muslims in the Middle East.

The women of Mali were much more visible than their Middle Eastern counterparts, in more ways than one. Mali women were more actively involved in their society and it wasn't uncommon to see female servants topless.

The kings of Mali could also be quite conspicuous in their displays of wealth.

This was the kingdom that Mansa Musa was born into and as a member of the nobility, he had certain rights and privileges that most didn't have.

Mansa Musa ascended to the throne in what can only be described as a twist of fate. Often it is unforeseen twists of fate like this that put heroes in a position to succeed and in Mansa Musa's case, it was an apparent tragedy that was the catalyst.

The ruling king of Mali led an expedition to explore the Atlantic Ocean, which left Mansa Musa in charge of the kingdom. When the King did not return, Mansa Musa was declared the new king. Once he was officially crowned, Mansa Musa wasted no time making a name for himself around the world.

Building Timbuktu

You've probably heard the name Timbuktu at some point in your life. Sure, the name sounds funny, so much so that a 1980s new wave band adopted it, but in the Middle Ages it was a center of culture in the Islamic world.

The Mali Empire sat on top of a large reserve in gold, perhaps one of the largest in the world at the time. Although the gold had little value within Mali, Mansa Musa knew that it was coveted by the Berbers, Arabs, and Europeans to the north. The people of the north wanted Mali's gold, and Mansa Musa wanted the knowledge of the Arabs and Berbers, so he developed regular caravan routes with North Africa.

As the gold left Mali, scholars entered the kingdom with knowledge of writing, science, architecture, and other ideas that were needed to develop a thriving kingdom. In no time, Timbuktu became a model African city, with the famed Djinguereber Mosque as the focal point. Besides building Timbuktu into a world-class city, Mansa Musa also used his wealth to help the poor, sick, and orphans of his kingdom. But it was his pilgrimage to Mecca that made him famous.

It's one of the Five Pillars of Islam that every pious Muslim should visit the holy city of Mecca at least one time in his or her life, so Mansa Musa began his journey in 1324 and returned to Mali a year later.

The Arab writers chronicled Mansa Musa's journey, the details of which still seem amazing.

The caravan included more than 60,000 Malians, 12,000 of which were slaves, each carrying a four-pound gold bar. In addition to the gold bars, 80 camels carried hundreds of pounds of gold dust each. Other exotic commodities the caravan brought included silk, ebony, and numerous fruits. The caravan gave gold dust to the poor along the route and when it made official stops at the palaces of sultans, gold bars were given as a token of friendship.

Mansa Musa injected so much gold into the kingdoms of the Middle East that it created an inflationary cycle that lasted for several decades!

Mansa Musa is often referred to as the wealthiest man in the world, but perhaps he should also be considered the most generous man in the world and the world's first philanthropist. Mansa Musa was truly a rich man, but he used his wealth to help his people, which makes him a genuine hero in many people's eyes.

DID YOU KNOW?

- There are conflicting reports on the exact year when Mansa Musa died, although most believe he died of natural causes. He was succeeded on the throne by his son, Maghan.

- Sankore University was the premier educational institute at the time and was generously funded by Mansa Musa. The curriculum included Islamic and Qur'anic studies, along with grammar, history, math, and science.

- Besides Timbuktu, there were as many as 400 cities in the Mali Empire, primarily centered in the Niger Delta.

- Due to Mansa Musa's travels, the Mali Empire was included in the Spanish Catalan Atlas of 1375. Word of the King and the empire slowly spread throughout Europe, but by the 7th century, it had collapsed and it became a mystery once more to those outside of Africa.

- The Great Mosque still stands in Timbuktu and is a protected UNESCO site. It was even considered a finalist in the New7Wonders of the World due to its unique architectural style and historical significance. The palace where Mansa Musa and the other Mali kings lived, though, is yet to be located in modern times.

CHAPTER 13

NELSON MANDELA: FROM WARFARE TO RECONCILIATION

You probably know at least a couple of things about late South African leader Nelson Mandela. You probably know that he resisted the system of government in South African known as apartheid, which was one where the White minority ruled over the Black majority. You also probably know that Mandela spent 27 years in prison for his resistance efforts, but once he was released, he was an international celebrity, sensation, and genuine Black hero.

But did you know that Mandela was descended from African tribal royalty?

Did you know that Mandela studied to be a lawyer during a time and in a place where few Blacks were allowed to practice the law?

Did you know that the world of South African politics that Mandela navigated was much more complex than simply Blacks against Whites?

All of these points factored into the epic journey that became Nelson Mandela's life. Mandela began his life as a relatively privileged kid from the Cape Province but moved to the big city, where he found most doors closed to him due to his race…Yet the path to political activism called him very loudly.

Once he decided to become an activist in the 1940s, Nelson dove headlong into organizing, making it his full-time job. He made several friends and allies along the way, but also earned the ire of the South African government and was jailed numerous times. After what seemed to be numerous failures in his battle against the South African government's apartheid policy, Mandela finally made the fateful decision to support a violent struggle against the government.

The decision landed him in prison for a good share of his adult life, but it also brought him international fame and brought pressure on South Africa to change its policies.

Slowly but surely, South Africa changed and when Mandela was released from prison, it seemed he too had changed.

Mandela no longer advocated armed resistance and instead called for reconciliation.

Once he became South Africa's first Black president and the first president democratically-elected by a majority of the country's population in 1994, it was clear that he was a changed man from his years of resistance and prison. He argued that people should learn from the past, but not live in it, and should instead move into the future.

Noble Origins

Despite being born in a country where his race automatically set him at a disadvantage, Mandela began his life with more privilege than the vast majority of South Africa's Black population. Born Rolihlahla Mandela on July 18, 1928, the future president was part of the Thembu people's nobility.

He was given a Western education, developed a love of history and the law, and took the Western name "Nelson" to fit in better in the world of the White man.

Mandela first studied at the all-Black University of Fort Hare in the Eastern Cape Province before moving to the other side of the country to Johannesburg in 1940. Nelson made the move for purely practical reasons, hoping to earn a law degree, but once he enrolled in the University of the Witwatersrand in Johannesburg, which was racially mixed but overwhelmingly White, Mandela was introduced to a whole new world.

While at Witwatersrand, Mandela became acquainted with communist and Marxist ideology and also formed lasting friendships with members of the African National Congress (ANC) and the South African Communist Party.

Mandela wished to take the ANC and affiliated organizations in a multi-racial left-wing direction that would use nonviolent tactics to affect change in South Africa. The young activist was able to draw a large number of followers from among the townships and shantytowns of South Africa, partially due to their dire situations, but also due to Mandela's natural charm and charisma.

One thing that many heroes have in common is an uncanny ability to influence people.

There is little doubt that Nelson Mandela had that "it" factor.

Mandela reached the peak of his pre-prison political and social success in the 1950s. He helped organize numerous anti-apartheid marches and campaigns, such as the 1951 Defiance Campaign, while running one of the only successful Black law firms in the country. Nelson could have chosen to focus on his law practice and become a wealthy individual away from the watchful eyes of the South African security forces, but he instead decided to live the dangerous and unstable life of a revolutionary.

And after many arrests and no noticeable changes in government policy - if anything, apartheid laws became stricter in the 1950s and '60s - Mandela made the momentous decision to turn to violent resistance.

The decision came when he was on the run due to a 1956 treason charge. As he still secretly met members of the international press in the late 1950s, Mandela was also forming the guerilla insurgency group Umkhonto we Sizwe, "Spear of the Nation" (abbreviated as "MK", which became the armed wing of the ANC). The MK was responsible for numerous bombings, targeted assassinations, and acts of sabotage in the late 1950s, which made Mandela public enemy #1.

Mandela was finally captured in 1962, possibly after an ANC member informed of his location to the police, or maybe due to CIA involvement. He was convicted of the original treason charge and given five years in prison, but the government discovered his involvement with the MK, and eventually he was sentenced to life in prison.

This is when Nelson Mandela truly became an international icon.

Reconciling the Past

Mandela would spend the next 27 years in a series of South African prisons, among them the notorious Robben Island prison. But, as much as possible, he didn't let prison slow down his activities. He occasionally received visits from supporters, wrote essays about South Africa that were later published, and became the hero of young Western leftists by the late 1960s.

By the early 1980s, "Free Mandela" was a slogan that could be heard across college campuses, in popular music, and seen on t-shirts in the United Kingdom, the United States, France, and just about every Western country.

For their part, the South African government took a hard stance against resistance to apartheid in the 1970s and into the 1980s, but by the end of the decade, things were beginning to change around the globe.

The communist world was collapsing, and although apartheid South Africa was opposed to the communist bloc, it had probably suffered even more due to its isolation. Many Western countries had economic sanctions against South Africa due to its apartheid policies, and it was, for the most part, banned from participating in the Olympics, FIFA World Cup, and many other international sports competitions.

In February 1990, the South African government's ban on the ANC was lifted and Nelson Mandela was finally released from prison. The relieved activist met with leaders of the ANC and thousands of his supporters. He urged peace but didn't rule out the use of violence if need be, which didn't thrill South African President F.W. de Klerk.

Mandela then embarked on a whirlwind tour of the world, meeting with leaders such as American President George H.W. Bush, laying out his plan for a post-apartheid South Africa. But Mandela was faced with a situation that was daunting, to say the least.

Mandela knew that if he didn't get a majority of South Africans - Black, White, Indian, and Colored (as the multi-racial ethnic group there is known) - to go along with his plan, then it'd never succeed.

Since the Whites held power in 1992, it was they who had to agree to share it with the other groups. In March 1992, a referendum was held to determine whether they (White South Africans only) should proceed with the process to dismantle the apartheid system.

A clear majority of 68% voted "yes," sending the message that apartheid was on its last legs. The first multi-racial elections were held in 1994, making Mandela president, but the South African leader's incredible story was not quite done.

In what many people see as proof of Mandela's enduring humanity, after his victory, instead of gloating and possibly punishing those who opposed him, he offered an olive branch. The Truth and Reconciliation Commission (TWC) was established in 1995 in Cape Town, South Africa to deal directly with South Africa's brutal legacy in a way that accepted its violent past while looking to the future. Those accused of apartheid-era crimes, of all races and political persuasions, were required to testify publicly regarding their crimes and, in return, be given amnesty.

The TWC is cited by many experts as a major reason why South Africa avoided a complete race/civil war in the 1990s, and it has served as a template for similar commissions around the world.

When Nelson Mandela died in 2013, he was remembered as many different things by many different people. He was seen as a courageous freedom fighter by some, a prisoner of conscience by others, and a magnanimous and empathetic man by others still.

The reality is, though, that Nelson Mandela embodied all of these traits and was all of these things during his long and eventful life, which makes him one of the greatest Black heroes of the 20th century.

DID YOU KNOW?

- During the height of his notoriety in the early 1990s, Mandela was often accompanied by his wife Winnie, his second wife. Nelson and Winnie were married from 1958 until 1996. He married his third and final wife, Graca, in 1998 at the age of 80. Nelson had six children with his first two wives.

- All of Mandela's friends, and most of his personal contacts, were Black until he moved to Johannesburg. When he worked with the South African Communist Party, Mandela befriended many Jewish activists, including Joe Slovo.

- Tribal and ethnic politics complicated Mandela's work and the peace process in South Africa overall. Although the Inkatha Freedom Party was a Black organization, it opposed the ANC and Mandela for several reasons: its members were primarily of the Zulu tribe, it favored a policy of racial separation, and it was anti-communist. The White population was also divided at the time. The more urban English-speaking population favored ending apartheid, while many in the more conservative Afrikaans-speaking community didn't.

- South African President Pik Botha offered to release Mandela from prison in 1985 if he "unconditionally rejected violence." He refused and pointed out that as long as the ANC was still banned, then it was a meaningless gesture.

- Nelson Mandela died on December 5, 2013 at the age of 95 in his home in Johannesburg. His body was interred in the Mandela family cemetery near the village of Qunu, Eastern Cape, South

CHAPTER 14

HARRIET TUBMAN: RUNNING THE UNDERGROUND RAILROAD

In American history, the era before the Civil War was characterized by westward expansion, European immigration, and of course, slavery. The British brought the institution of slavery with them over to North America and for a time, it was widely practiced in all 13 of the original American colonies and even in what is now Canada.

The situation persisted after American independence, although the states north of the Mason-Dixon Line (the border between Virginia and Maryland that delineated free states from slave states) gradually abolished slavery. There were multiple reasons why slavery was abolished in the North: liberal anti-slavery and abolitionist sentiments were common, although not the majority; but more importantly, the Northern economy just didn't rely on the labor system of slavery.

On the other hand, as the American republic expanded westward, new lands in the south opened that were prime locations for growing cotton, tobacco, rice, and sugar. All of these were labor-intensive crops and many of them were grown in regions that people of African descent were purportedly more adaptable toward than Europeans in terms of handling extreme heat and malaria.

Slave rebellions were rare and the exception, not the rule. But slaves absconding from their bondage was fairly common.

As the sectional differences between the North and South grew in the 1840s, many Northern politicians and leaders encouraged slaves to abscond from their masters, which led to fiery debates, accusations, and political fights in Washington, D.C. Northern White abolitionists began aiding escaped slaves, helping them secure their freedom.

But not all of those helping escaped slaves find freedom in the North and beyond, were White.

Some slaves and former slaves took the extra risk of helping fellow slaves find freedom in the North and Canada. After the passage of the Fugitive Slave Act of 1850, White abolitionists caught helping slaves escape to freedom could face fines or jail time, but for a slave or former slave to get caught, it would usually mean something much worse.

Harriet Tubman was a former slave who took the great risk of helping former slaves find freedom in the North, not once or twice, but 13 times. Tubman became one of the legendary Underground Railroad's top conductors, helping more than 70 slaves find the promised land. Once the Civil War began, she used her knowledge and networks to help the Union Army.

Tubman appeared unassuming and harmless, which allowed her to pull off incredible mission's right under the noses of countless slave catchers. During her life, Tubman became a heroine to thousands of former slaves and in the century since her death, her fame and impact on modern society have only grown.

A Complex Life

Tubman was born Araminta Ross to slave parents in the state of Maryland sometime between 1815 and 1825. Of course, being born into slavery was bad, but conditions for slaves varied based on their status and their owners. Slaves who worked in the owner's home and those with technical skills usually fared better than those who were relegated to working in the fields. However, although Tubman worked primarily in the homes of her owners and of people her owners hired her out to, she did not escape mistreatment.

Since Araminta was physically strong, she was eventually used for field work, which is where she was introduced to some of the more brutal aspects of slavery.

In one particularly harsh incident, Harriet was accidentally struck in the head by a metal bar that the overseer was attempting to use on a fleeing slave. The head injury proved to be quite traumatic, leaving Tubman with headaches and blurred vision for the remainder of her life.

Despite generally growing up in a difficult and precarious position, unlike many slaves, Tubman knew and often lived with her family. She was also allowed to marry a Black freedman named John Tubman in 1844. Not long after she married John, Araminta changed her name to Harriet and began to take on an entirely new persona.

She became much more religious and claimed to have had visions, which may have been the result of her traumatic head injury, although it is difficult to judge a person's mystical experiences. Harriet also became more assertive and independent, eventually fleeing with her brothers Ben and Harry on September 17, 1849.

The escape proved to be somewhat of a failure. Harriet's brothers decided to turn back, so she went with them and although she found herself in slavery again, the short jaunt to temporary freedom proved to her that it was possible.

So Harriet Tubman decided to make the five-day journey into Pennsylvania and freedom by herself.

Guided only by the North Star, Harriet traveled through wooded areas and pastures at night and slept during the day in barns and sheds owned by abolitionist members of the Underground Railroad.

Once safely in Philadelphia, Tubman could have begun a new life and few would have blamed her.

But one of the things that all the heroes and heroines in this book had was a meaningful commitment to self-sacrifice and altruism.

Harriet Tubman was dedicated to freeing the rest of her family and as many others as possible, especially after the Fugitive Slave Act of 1850 was passed.

Tubman made use of the elaborate network of abolitionists and slaves known as the Underground Railroad to brings scores of slaves to freedom. She carried a pistol, not only in case slavecatchers caught her, but also to intimidate any slaves she was leading who thought about turning back— doing so would jeopardize an entire mission and possibly the entire Underground Railroad.

By the late 1850s, Tubman was leading slaves into Canada, as the Fugitive Slave Act allowed slavecatchers free reign in Northern, free states. Numerous bounties were placed on Tubman's capture, but like a panther, she continued to elude her captors. By the time the Civil War started, Tubman boasted of a perfect record on her missions.

Tubman's record was so good that she came to the attention of the Union Army during the Civil War.

Scouting for the Union Army

When the Civil War broke out in 1861, the Union/North didn't immediately make it about Blacks or ending slavery. For the Confederacy, the preservation of slavery was a paramount concern, but for the North, the primary issue was preserving the Union; if that meant letting the South have slavery, then so be it. Lincoln didn't issue the Emancipation Proclamation until 1863, and before that, most in the North thought very little about the topic of slavery.

And that included Blacks who volunteered to help the Union's war effort.

Tubman immediately offered to help the Union with intelligence in the border areas and possibly with helping organize former slaves, but her gestures were met rather coldly at first, to say the least. So, Tubman worked as a nurse for the two years of the war, but when Lincoln issued the Emancipation Proclamation, things changed.

The Proclamation led to a massive wave of slave refugees headed north, many of whom wanted to fight. Fighting also became more intense in northern Virginia in 1863, which led many Union officers to see the military value in Tubman's networks.

Tubman began scouting for the Union Army in northern Virginia, providing valuable intelligence that helped win numerous battles.

Unfortunately, though, since Tubman was a former slave, and a woman, it was easy for many to ignore her accomplishments and help. Tubman was never recognized or paid by the government for her service, although the abolitionist community supported her throughout the rest of her life.

Harriet Tubman lived out her days in upstate New York, a legend in her own time. She continued to be politically active in the suffragette movement until she died on March 10, 1913.

DID YOU KNOW?

- Harriet divorced her first husband in 1851. She remarried a Black Union Army veteran named Nelson Davis after the war.

- As her fame as an Underground Railroad conductor preceded her, she earned the nickname "Moses" —who, of course, led the Israelites out of captivity in Egypt, according to the book of Exodus in the Bible.

- Tubman became friends with legendary White abolitionist John Brown in the late 1850s. Tubman is said to have helped Brown plan his ill-fated raid on Harper's Ferry in 1859, but for reasons that aren't clear, she did not participate. If she had, she would've surely been executed, which raises the question of just how well-known she would be today if that had occurred.

- While Tubman was riding on a train in New York state in 1869, the conductor physically removed her to the baggage car. Her refusal to go is often cited as the inspiration for Rosa Park's protest on a Montgomery bus in 1955.

- Although Harriet Tubman's legacy is, for the most part, not controversial today, calls for her to replace President Andrew Jackson on the $20 have been met with plenty of resistance. The matter remains undecided.

CHAPTER 15

BEN CARSON: MEDICAL PIONEER

It should be clear to you by now that the backgrounds of the world's Black heroes and heroines are as diverse and varied as their numbers. We've met both men and women who have inspired countless numbers in fields such as sports and entertainment, politics and government, and warfare and the military.

We've also met heroes and heroines from three different continents ranging over more than 2,000 years of human history. Many of these heroes and heroines were larger than life and truly enjoyed basking in the limelight, but a few made incredible contributions to humanity and were quite humble in doing so.

Doctor Ben Carson is one such man.

You may know Ben Carson as a 2016 Republican presidential candidate who later became the Secretary of Housing and Urban Development in the Cabinet of President Donald Trump, but he had an entirely separate career before that.

Long before Carson even entertained the idea of entering politics, he was a world-renowned neurosurgeon who saved countless lives and performed some pretty incredible surgeries. For example, Carson is the only surgeon who has ever successfully separated twins conjoined at the back of their heads, which he did in 1987.

Carson then imparted his knowledge to the medical and scientific communities by performing more surgeries, assisting other surgeons in procedures, and by publishing his ideas and discoveries in numerous articles, and books and by giving many speeches and television appearances.

The humble and usually softly-spoken Carson segued into politics in 2013, where he continues to be positive role model and a true Black hero to countless people around the world.

Dealing with a Deep Rage

Carson's early life can best be summarized in one word—instability. He was born Benjamin Solomon Carson on September 18, 1951, to an army veteran father and a very religious mother. Carson's mother, Sonya, had a much bigger impact on his life than his father did, raising him and his brother in the Seventh Day Adventist Church and severely regimented their television habits.

As much as Ben's mother cared for him and his brother, though, things were difficult for her.

Ben's father, Robert, was discovered to be a bigamist, which led Sonya to divorce him, setting off a period of instability for Ben. Sonya moved her family to different neighborhoods of Detroit and briefly to Boston, Massachusetts. Sonya also struggled with mental illness during the 1950s and into the 1960s, which adversely effected Ben.

Feeling isolated with no father figure, and often not knowing how long he'd live in a particular house or neighborhood, Ben often lashed out violently at his friends and family. He was routinely involved in fights in high school, occasionally attacked other kids with rocks and sticks, and even once attacked his mother with a hammer.

But according to Carson, the turning point came when he attempted to stab one of his friends with a knife.

Carson claims that he tried to stab the kid, but his friend's belt buckle stopped the blade from doing any damage. It was at that point that Carson acknowledged he had a rage problem. He believed God was watching over him by stopping the blade. Ben immediately went home, prayed to God, and vowed to never hurt another human.

He improved his grades and became active in extra-curricular activities, developing a particular aptitude for public speaking. Along with a good SAT score, it was all enough to land Carson at Yale in the late 1960s.

America was going through incredible changes at the time, but Carson was only interested in how he could help people. By 1973, Ben Carson had transformed the rage of his childhood into a burning desire to become a doctor.

Seeing Things Differently

Carson returned to his home state, graduating from the University of Michigan Medical School in 1977. Medical school wasn't always easy for Ben, but by then he knew how to overcome adversity and even use it to his advantage. Carson decided to specialize in neurosurgery, which is among the most difficult of all medical disciplines. A neurosurgeon doesn't just need to have plenty of knowledge; they also must have steady hands and an ability to see things differently.

Ben Carson has the unique ability to see a problem as a three-dimensional image.

Working at John Hopkins University in Maryland, Carson began saving the lives of countless patients, but of course, the operation that brought him international fame was when he successfully separated Patrick and Benjamin Binder in 1987. Although Patrick survived only in a vegetative state for more than 20 years and Benjamin survived with neurological damage, the operation was considered a major step forward by the medical and scientific communities.

The knowledge gained from the operation was used to successfully separate Zambian conjoined twins Joseph and Luka Banda in 1997. The Banda brothers were also joined at the back of their heads, but Carson was able to use his experience to ensure that both not only lived but that they didn't suffer any permanent neurological damage.

The world of neurosurgery is, for the most part, a young person's game, so in 2013, Carson retired to focus on publications, public speaking, and politics. But Carson quickly found that the political world was much more cut throat than he'd expected, so he withdrew from the presidential race in support of future President Trump.

Ben Carson continues to exert his softly-spoken but respected influence on government policy, largely behind the scenes. Carson may not be the flashiest or most headline-grabbing hero in our book, but few can deny the impact that he's had on the world.

DID YOU KNOW?

- Cuba Gooding Junior played Ben Carson in the 2009 biopic *Gifted Hands: The Ben Carson Story*. The film chronicles some of the ups and downs of Carson's early life, culminating with his decision to operate on the Binder twins in 1987.

- As part of his preparation for the operation on the Binder twins, Carson had two dolls conjoined that he and his 70-member team studied for weeks before the surgery.

- Carson married his wife Lacena in 1975. They are still married and have three children.

- Carson was awarded the Presidential Medal of Freedom for his work in medicine by President George W. Bush in 2008.

- Despite being a prominent member of the Republican Party today, Carson was a Democrat until

CHAPTER 16

BARACK OBAMA: YES WE CAN

Unless you've been living in a cave for the last 20 years, you know that Barack Obama was the United States' 44th president for two terms from January 20, 2009 to January 20, 2017. Before being elected president, Obama served half a term as US Senator from the state of Illinois, and as a member of the Illinois Senate from January 8, 1997 to November 4, 2004.

Of course, what made Obama's run historic, and made him a genuine Black hero to millions of Americans, was the fact that he became the United States' first Black president. Born to a White American mother and a Kenyan father on August 4, 1961, Obama certainly didn't seem "destined" to be the future president of the United States.

The closest any Black politician had come to the highest office in the land was Jesse Jackson's run for the Democrat Party's presidential nomination in 1984, which he lost to Walter Mondale, who was defeated in a landslide by President Ronald Reagan.

And during that 1984 election cycle, popular African-American comedian Eddie Murphy basically summed up the situation in his October 24, 1983 HBO standup special, *Eddie Murphy Delirious*:

"I've seen him (Jesse Jackson) running around the track and shit. I said why the fuck you getting in shape Jesse?"

"Because I'm going to be the first black president. I have to give speeches like this" (Murphy then runs back and forth across the stage).

Good comedy is often a reflection on contemporary society, and in 1983, which wasn't *too* long ago, most people just didn't think America would see a Black president anytime soon. Yes, some thought that assassination would be a real possibility, but most just thought that "the country wasn't ready for it."

Barack Obama proved everyone wrong when he ran and won in 2008.

Laying Roots around the World

Obama's childhood and upbringing in many ways prepared him for the life and career he would later have, as he traveled extensively, made extensive contacts, and developed a more global worldview. Barack Hussein Obama was born in Hawaii, which is also where he spent his formative years.

Although racially mixed, which was quite rare at the time in the United States, Hawaii was a different story. It had only been a state for a few years. Young Obama played with kids from a variety of different backgrounds, which complemented the multi-national and multi-ethnic background of his extended family, which he once referred to as a "little mini-United Nations."

But as idyllic as Hawaii may have been for Obama in some ways, his early life did have its share of difficulties.

Barack's parents divorced in 1964, leaving him with virtually no relationship with his father. He would only see his father once before he died in a car accident in 1982.

Obama struggled at times with fitting in, his ethnic identity, and his overall place in the world. After his mother remarried, to an Indonesian man, she took Barack with her on travels throughout Asia, expanding the young man's perceptions about the world.

After seeing how small he was in the big scheme of things, and just how much there was in the world still to see, Obama endeavored to do his utmost to learn more about the world and to help make it better when and where he could. He was accepted into the prestigious Occidental College in California on a scholarship in 1979 and later transferred to the equally prestigious Columbia, where he earned a BA in 1983.

Obama worked as a community organizer in poor, predominantly Black neighborhoods in Chicago and other cities throughout the 1980s, which helped him gain experience and more importantly, vital political contacts. After earning a law degree from Harvard University in 1991, Obama returned to Chicago intent on using his knowledge to affect positive change in his adopted hometown.

By the late 1990s, for many native Illinoisans, Barack Obama was synonymous with the city of Chicago.

Obama and the Windy City

Obama put the connections he made in Chicago during the 1980s to good use in the 1990s. Few would argue against the notion that Chicago politics is a tough business, as labor unions, the Democrat Party political machine, and ethnic voting blocs hold sway.

There's also no denying that organized crime has its influence on the city's politics.

The generally laid-back and peaceful Obama—who was raised in Hawaii, remember—had to learn a new skill-set to deal with these people. So, how was Obama able to do it?

Well, Barack Obama was often one of the smarter people in the room, and when he wasn't, he was often the most charismatic. Obama had an uncanny ability to relate to people from a wide range of backgrounds, probably owing to his youth in Hawaii and traveling the world with his mother. This was true even with people who didn't necessarily like him at first due to his background and looks.

And once Obama had a captive audience, he was able to further persuade and inspire them with his loquacious speaking abilities.

After serving in the state senate and winning several influential allies in the state capital of Springfield, Obama decided to run for the open US Senate seat in 2004. Illinois is today a reliably Democrat, "blue" state, and mostly was in 2004, but it still wasn't as blue as California or New York. Illinois has plenty of Republicans, "red" counties and congressional districts in the central and southern part of the state, with Chicago's suburbs vacillating politically. Therefore, Obama would need to campaign in every region of the state to win.

Obama won the Democrat Party's nomination easily and was slated to compete against Republican businessman Jack Ryan in what was expected to be a close election.

But then, as often does with many heroes and heroines in history, fate made an appearance.

Ryan was going through a bitter custody battle with his wife, actress Jeri Ryan, and when it was revealed through court documents that he liked to take his wife to sex clubs, it ruined any chances he had of beating Obama. The Republicans quickly added Black conservative Alan Keyes as a replacement, but it was too little too late.

Obama won the election in a landslide, setting up his run for the presidency.

As the American economy crumbled in late 2008, Obama was poised to be elected as an answer—and as a breath of fresh air after the Bush years. Putting together a diverse political coalition, as he had done in Illinois, Obama rode a wave of enthusiasm to an easy presidential victory in 2008 and a slightly less easy, yet still impressive, reelection in 2012.

Throughout his two terms as president, Obama advocated many politically liberal policies, with his signature political victory being the passage of the Affordable Care Act, more commonly known as "Obama Care," in 2010.

Like most presidents, Obama experienced many highs and lows during his presidency, comforted the people during tragedies, and stood as a symbol of a new America in the world. But probably more important than any policy he advocated, or any bill he signed into law, Barack Obama is seen as a hero for the potential he represented and his ability to inspire others.

DID YOU KNOW?

- Obama married Chicago native Michelle Robinson in 1992. They have two daughters, Malia and Natasha.

- Barack's mother, Stanley Ann Dunham, died in 1995 of ovarian cancer at the age of 52. As Barack's mother was often traveling and his father was out of the picture, Stanley Ann's parents, Stanley and Madelyn, helped raise Obama in his early years.

- Obama has a half-sister, Maya Soetoro-Ng, from his mother and her second husband, Lolo Soetoro. He also had seven half-siblings through his father.

- Although Obama ran on a platform of ending American military interventions around the world and pulling American troops out of Iraq, this didn't eventuate. By the end of his second term, American troops in Iraq had increased, drone strikes were being authorized in Yemen, and it was announced that troops would be stationed in Afghanistan indefinitely.

- Obama wrote two books that were published before he was elected president: *Dreams from My Father* (1995) and *The Audacity of Hope* (2006).

CHAPTER 17

GEORGE WASHINGTON CARVER: MODERN RENAISSANCE MAN

The term "Renaissance man" gets thrown around a lot today without most people knowing what it is classifying. The term began its usage in the years after the period in European history known as the Renaissance—roughly the mid-1400s to the mid to late 1500s - to refer to some of the many intellectual heavyweights that were prominent in that era. Men such as

Leonard da Vinci, Donatello, and countless others, blessed the world with their art as well as literature and science.

Another word for a Renaissance man is a polymath, but that just doesn't sound as poetic, does it?

In the centuries after the Renaissance (and before it) there have been thousands of men and women who could fit the definition of a Renaissance man or polymath. American history is full of plenty, especially early American history. Thomas Jefferson and Benjamin Franklin are perhaps the United States' two greatest Renaissance Men. Both men were fluent in multiple languages, were engaged in politics and government, and were also able scientists in their own rights.

About 100 years after Franklin and Jefferson made their mark on the world, a true Renaissance man named George Washington Carver was doing the same in the American South.

Carver became famous for his contributions to American agriculture, particularly his promotion of the peanut as a major cash crop in the South. During his life, Washington also proved to be a gifted artist, teacher, researcher, and public speaker. This is all incredible in and of itself; but Carver achieved all of this in the late 1800's and early 1900's in the segregated South. By rising above the limitations placed in front of him, George Washington Carver proved to be a true American and one of the most brilliant of all Black heroes.

An Intense Drive to Learn

George Washington Carver was born into slavery sometime just before the start of the Civil War in Southwest Missouri. He was owned by a man named Moses Carver, and like most former slaves, took his owner's surname after the war.

George had to travel great distances as a child to enroll and attend at schools that took Black students, but from an early age, he knew that education was the key to success, so he did whatever he could to stay in school. He was mostly fascinated by biology and other sciences, but he also enjoyed reading about history. During his teens or twenties, he took the middle name Washington, probably in honor of the nation's first president.

Perhaps somewhat ironically, his early life closely followed the same pattern of another Black hero named Washington, Booker T. Washington. The lives and fortunes of both men would be closely connected for several years.

But we'll get more to that a bit later.

Carver's desire to learn couldn't be contained, so he applied to several colleges, but he was repeatedly rejected due to his race. Undeterred by the rejections, Carver began conducting agricultural experiments on some land he bought in Kansas, which became the basis for much of his later research. He was particularly impressed with peanuts and their ability to grow in the climate of the American South. Carver eventually developed hundreds of products and recipes for peanuts, although he didn't actually invent the one he is most famous for - peanut butter.

As Carver worked his Kansas farm and did his research, he received a letter of acceptance to Simpson College in Iowa in 1890. Carver studied art and piano at Simpson and then transferred to Iowa State Agricultural College (now Iowa State University) to study botany.

Although he was the only Black student in his class and the first at Iowa State, Carver excelled in his studies and got along quite well with his professors and fellow students. Carver earned a BA from Iowa State in 1894 and an MS in 1896.

The year 1896 would also be the year that two of the greatest Black thinkers in history came together.

Carver and Washington

By 1896, George Washington Carver's academic reputation proceeded him. He was regarded as not only one of the greatest Black academics of the era but also one of the greatest thinkers of the time. White academics invited him to speak at lectures and conferences where White farmers listened intently to his theories on crop rotation, sweet potato farming, and how peanuts restore nitrogen to soil.

Carver was certainly an academic and intellectual giant at the time, so Booker T. Washington recruited him to teach and do research at the Tuskegee Institute in 1896.

George would spend the rest the remainder of his life teaching, conducting research, and publishing his findings from his lab and office in Tuskegee, but things weren't always easy.

Due to his academic reputation, Carver was given much more money and attention than the other teachers at Tuskegee, in addition to being given his own living quarters, office, and laboratory. The treatment created resentment within some of the faculty towards Carver, but Washington didn't care. He knew that George Washington Carver was a 'once-in-a-lifetime' type genius who could make or break the Tuskegee Institute.

So, Washington did everything in his power to make Carver happy.

With that said, though, Washington and Carver butted heads plenty of times. As both men were legends in their own time, it was probably inevitable that they would do this; and as much as they were similar as notable Black heroes who were close contemporaries, they also had very different personalities and attitudes.

Washington was known for being an extroverted, gregarious, and charismatic person; while Carver was friendly, he largely kept to himself and had few close friends or relationships throughout his life.

Both Carver and Washington were excellent teachers, but where Washington excelled in administration, Carver was weak. Carver was, above all, a true research academic and like many true researchers, he felt that the administrative side of academia was a waste of his talents.

He was probably right. And for the most part, Washington seemed to know that too and often relented.

After Washington died, Carver was given a much wider reign at Tuskegee and was able to devote almost all of his time to research and teaching. Carver continued to work until he died in 1943, having made the world a notably better - and you could say better tasting - place!

DID YOU KNOW?

- In 1921, during the height of segregation and Jim Crow laws, Carver testified before Congress on behalf of peanut farmers to argue for a tariff on imported peanuts as a result, a tariff on imported peanuts was passed a year later.

- As an example of how famous Carver was during his life, and how his fame transcended race, he appeared on a 1948 US postage stamp.

- In 1916, Carver's short book *How to Grow the Peanut and 105 Ways of Preparing it for Human Consumption* was published. It was seen as the gold standard of peanut farming for decades and much of it is still relevant today.

- Carver applied for and received several patents for peanut and sweet potato uses. Some of those uses include dyes, medicines, and instant coffee.

- Carver had the rare honor of meeting three sitting American presidents: Theodore Roosevelt, Calvin Coolidge, and Franklin Roosevelt. Again, this was incredible considering it was the era of racial segregation.

CHAPTER 18

FRANTZ FANON: CARIBBEAN ANTI-COLONIAL PHILOSOPHER

The next person in our book is among the lesser-known of all the heroes on our list and is not necessarily considered a hero by all those familiar with him. More Whites may revere Frantz Fanon today than Blacks, and most of those who do consider him a hero are college professors with a serious Marxist bent.

With that said, there is no denying that Frantz Fanon greatly influenced the course of history during and immediately after his death, with his ideas greatly contributing to the Third World Liberation Movement in the decades immediately after World War II. Long after he died of leukemia in 1961, Fanon's writings were cited as influences by leftist revolutionaries in Africa, Asia, and Latin America and by members of the Black Panthers in the United States.

Today, Fanon's writings are most widely disseminated in college philosophy and history classes.

But let's face it, writers and philosophers are a dime a dozen, right? So then, what made Frantz Fanon so important and a Black hero to so many people across the globe? Well, unlike the college professors who claim to support his ideas of "liberation" from their cozy faculty offices and gentrified urban or suburban neighborhoods, Fanon lived the life he promoted.

Fanon could have lived a life as comfortable as those of the countless college professors who lecture on their writings today. He could have been among the colonial elite in his native Martinique or he could have opened a lucrative medical practice in France that catered to the colonial diaspora. Instead, though, Fanon chose to fight in the Algerian War of Independence (1954-1962), placing his life in danger numerous times, and forgoing a life of comfort.

For many around the world who were involved in anti-colonial struggles and wars, Fanon was a hero because of his sacrifice. Most of those who knew of him had never read his books, but they were well aware of the name Frantz Fanon and the fact that he gave up plenty for a cause.

Colonialism First-Hand

Like many notable left-wing philosophers throughout history, Fanon wasn't born into poverty. He was raised in a comfortably middle-class family in the French Caribbean colony of Martinique, where he went to the best school on the island. Fanon's life trajectory was headed in a positive direction, on his way to possibly earning a nice living and becoming one of the island's colonial elites.

But in 1940 fate stepped in to change the trajectory of Fanon's life.

After Germany invaded France in World War II, the world's maps were immediately redrawn. The Germans occupied Northern France, but the southern part of the country, and all of its overseas colonies, were controlled by a pro-fascist, collaborationist government in the city of Vichy. The Vichy government controlled Martinique but were blockaded by the British, and later the American, navies.

The sudden turn of events put the 18-year-old Fanon in a curious position in 1943.

Fanon had always lived under the thumb of colonialism, but it was a sort of soft colonialism that he and most of his people considered benign for the most part. Once World War II broke out, though, and the Vichy government's political stance became more openly fascist, he saw first-hand that many French believed colonial citizens to be inferior.

Fanon fought for the Free French Army - they were the French who remained loyal to the original government and who supported the Allies - getting wounded in battle and receiving the *Croix de Guerre*. But he never felt he was given the proper respect owed to him and the other colonial soldiers.

It was in the waning years of World War II and just after that Fanon's political views took a hard left turn. He educated himself on Marxist philosophy and supported the French Communist Party in Martinique as he earned a BA. Then he was offered a scholarship to study medicine at the University of Lyon in France.

Frantz Fanon may have been a son of Martinique, but he would make his name elsewhere.

Scholar and Revolutionary

Fanon was awarded his scholarship as part of a wider push by the French government to educate the elite class of its colonies to prepare them to be leaders. It's somewhat ironic then that Fanon would take advantage of this situation and ultimately use it against the French.

Fanon specifically studied psychiatry, which allowed him to indulge in some of his other burgeoning academic pursuits. Influenced heavily by Marx, Freud, and others, Fanon began articulating the theory that colonial peoples saw their identity, even their worth, entirely from the perspective of their White-European rulers.

Frantz wrote about and later had these ideas published in the book *Black Skin, White Masks* in 1952. A year prior to that, Fanon had qualified and began practicing as a psychiatrist.

But Fanon was a restless soul and felt compelled to be where the action was.

After working in Algeria as a psychiatrist for a couple of years, Fanon was faced with another crossroads in his life when the Algerian War of Independence broke out in November 1954. On one side was the French government, which had ruled Algeria as a colony for nearly 100 years, and on the other side was the Front de Libération Nationale (FLN), which was an anti-colonial, leftist group that used a variety of guerilla tactics.

Fanon chose to join the FLN.

The war was difficult and cost Fanon dearly, but he was able to better develop his ideas for a specific anti-colonial audience. Fanon argued that violence was acceptable if it involved a colonial subaltern/oppressed people fighting against the colonial oppressor. Putting all of his ideas into print, along with some of the tactics and strategies he learned in war, Fanon wrote his magnum opus, *Les Damnés de la Terre* (*The Wretched of the Earth*), which was published just before his death in 1961.

Fanon's death was low-key and missed by much of the press, but by the late 1960s, his books and life had become well-known and quite influential throughout the world. From that point forward, Frantz Fanon was forever known as *the* anti-colonial philosopher and revolutionary. There have been countless writers and philosophers who have written anti-colonial screeds and a few successful anti-colonial revolutionaries, but Frantz Fanon was one of the only people in history to be a successful revolutionary *and* philosopher.

DID YOU KNOW?

- The details surrounding Frantz Fanon's death have been a subject of controversy for years. When he was fighting in Algeria, he sought treatment for leukemia in the Soviet Union but ended up dying at a US military hospital in Bethesda, Maryland. He was brought to the United States by the CIA and had a CIA handler, which has raised many questions. Some believe the US government was attempting to co-opt and control the anti-colonial movement through Fanon, while others suggest he was a CIA asset for some years before his death.

- Fanon married a French woman named Josie. The couple had a boy and a girl, both of whom are still alive and quite active in promoting their father's legacy in academia.

- Fanon argued that although racism and anti-Semitism were similar, they came from different perspectives. Anti-Semitism was a hatred of Jews for what they represent, while racism was a hatred of what could be seen physically, he wrote.

- *A Dying Colonialism* (1959) was Fanon's account of the Algerian War of Independence. Although the book contained plenty of Fanon's political theories, it is noted for relating many of the tactics the FLN used in its victory.

- Although he did not coin the terms, Frantz Fanon is often viewed as the father of 'critical theory' and 'critical race theory'.

CHAPTER 19

B.B. KING:
THE KING OF THE BLUES

We've already profiled a couple of notable Black music heroes in our book that truly pushed the boundaries and brought plenty of joy to millions of people around the world, making them true heroes in the process. But when it comes to American music, few Black musicians left a mark on the entertainment industry bigger than Riley "B.B." King.

The Mississippi born, Memphis, Tennessee adopted bluesman revolutionized the blues genre by developing a style that added new, modern elements, yet stayed true to the original.

As King began finding success in the business by producing albums and relentlessly touring, he brought the blues to a much wider audience. Before B.B. King, the blues was pretty much only played and listened to by the poor Blacks in the Deep South, but after B.B., everyone knew what the blues was.

B.B. King was also one of the driving forces behind the blues' rise in popularity in Europe and beyond.

But as talented as B.B. King was with a guitar, he was also a true ironman of the music business. From 1959 to 2008 King recorded more than 40 studio albums, 14 live albums, had scores of hit singles, and appeared on several compilations with other musicians.

He also toured non-stop, more than 300 days a year at his peak, and only retired from touring in 2014, just one year before he died at the age of 89.

B.B. King seemed to live the life of many Black heroes and heroines through his music: life is often tough and at times may seem hopeless, but if you can sing about it then you might just have a chance.

Learning to Sing the Blues

Riley King was born on September 16, 1925. in Leflore County, Mississippi, just about an hour south of the mythical "Crossroads" where legendary bluesman Robert Johnson supposedly sold his soul to the Devil to learn the art of the blues.

B.B. King didn't sell his soul to the Devil to learn the blues; he did it the hard way.

They say that for any musician to be a true bluesman, he has to *experience* the blues. Poverty, racism, violence, hunger, and heartbreak are among the many things cited as influences of the blues, and what gives the blues its soul.

Growing up in rural Mississippi, King experienced all of the above.

King was born into poverty in racially segregated Mississippi and to make things worse, his mother left their family when he was only four.

For many, such a situation would be insurmountable, but young Riley found solace in his local church, which is where he learned that he had a natural aptitude for music. He had a good voice, an ear for music, and was able to teach himself how to play the guitar and other instruments. Gospel is what he played in church and was the first style of music he learned, but he was instinctively drawn to the blues.

King knew from a young age that he wanted to be like Robert Johnson and some of the other first wave bluesmen, but there were few opportunities in rural Mississippi.

King made his way a couple of hours north to Memphis, Tennessee in 1946. The Beale Street neighborhood of Memphis, where bluesmen played nightly in dozens of bars, was the heart and soul of the Black community at the time.

Riley immediately made some connections, got some live gigs on Beale Streat, and landed a job as a disk jockey at WDIA, the first radio station in America dedicated to a Black audience. While working at WDIA, Riley became known as "Blues Boy King," which was later abbreviated to B.B. King.

By the early 1950s, everyone in Memphis knew about B.B. and Ike Turner introduced King to the important movers and shakers in town, including legendary music producer Sam Philips. By the mid-1950s he was recording numerous singles and doing live shows nearly every night.

There was no one bigger in Memphis by the end of the decade - except possibly Elvis Presley himself, and although Elvis may have been the King of Rock n' Roll, B.B. King had become the King of the Blues.

An International Sensation

The 1960s were very good for B.B. King's career. He signed a lucrative contract with major record label MCA and was able to take advantage of the changing social climate to further his name and career. As music and social ideas changed in the 1960s, many young people were going out of their way to listen to and learn more about blues, jazz, and other traditionally African-American music in a quest to be more "authentic."

And the kids liked what they heard from B.B. King!

King's mainstream popularity reached a peak when he opened for the Rolling Stones during their 1969 American tour. Then, in 1970, King was finally recognized by the wider American music community when he won a Grammy for the hit song, "The Thrill Is Gone." After that, King was pretty much a household name. Even people who didn't necessarily like the blues, or even know much about it, could recognize King playing his Gibson guitar.

The added fame just meant more work for King, who toured and recorded at an even more feverish pace.

But unlike many heroes and heroines who weren't recognized for their accomplishments in their lifetimes, B.B. was rightfully rewarded for being the greatest bluesman of the second wave of the blues. In 1980, King was inducted into the Blues Hall of Fame, followed by the Rock and Roll Hall of Fame in 1987, and the National Rhythm & Blues Hall of Fame in 2014.

Few American musicians have had such an enduring and influential career as King's, and fewer still have had such an incredible life story. Beginning life as a poor kid from rural Mississippi, King made a niche musical genre not only popular in his home country, but throughout the world. Today, some of the biggest bluesmen can be found in countries such as Ireland and Australia, which makes B.B. King one of the greatest Black music heroes in history.

DID YOU KNOW?

- King always played a Gibson ES-345-355 guitar. Although he went through several different guitars, he always named them "Lucille." He claimed that the name came from a 1949 incident at a juke joint in Arkansas. As he was playing a show, a fight broke out between two men that caused a fire. As the fire raged, King ran back inside to retrieve his guitar. He was later told that the men were fighting over a woman named Lucille.

- Unlike entertainers today, King stayed away from politics for the most part, although he was an advocate of prison reform. He recorded a live album in the Cook County Jail in Chicago, Illinois in 1970.

- King was married twice but had no children with either woman. One account claims that King's sperm count was too low to conceive children, but at least 15 people came forward during his lifetime claiming he was their father. He never denied any of the claims and offered financial support to all of the claimants.

- King was also a bit of an actor, appearing in minor and cameo roles in several television shows and movies, including *Sanford and Son*, *The Cosby Show*, and the 1998 film, *Blues Brothers 2000*.

- Later in his life, he became an entrepreneur, capitalizing on his name by opening B.B. King's Blues Clubs around the country. The first club opened on Beale Street in Memphis in 1994, with other clubs opening around the country in later years.

CHAPTER 20

54TH MASSACHUSETTS: FIGHTING FOR THEIR FREEDOM

We've already touched on how complex the American Civil War was and how it meant different things to different people. Yes, the war was essentially about the institution of slavery in America, but the degree to which either side fought for or against the "peculiar institution" varied widely. The Confederacy was more invested in preserving slavery as it was felt that it was crucial to its economy, but the reality is that most men fighting in the Confederate Army didn't own slaves.

It's also true that the Northern states were politically opposed to the spread of slavery, but the reality is that most men fighting in the Union Army were far from being racial egalitarians.

In other words, for most involved in the Civil War, it was a very gray affair (yes, pun intended).

So when the idea of the army organizing freed Blacks into "colored" regiments in the North began being proposed, most thought the idea was preposterous or even offensive. To some in the North, the war between the states was a war between brothers, and adding freedmen and other Blacks into the mix would only serve to harm the relationship more than it already had been. These people wanted to do whatever they could to bring the Southern states back into the Union as painlessly as possible and, in their view, arming Blacks would only complicate the healing process.

Others believed that Black soldiers were incapable of fighting. They thought that it was a waste of time and resources to train Blacks to fight because they couldn't be disciplined, could turn on their officers, and more than likely would flee when the shooting began.

But not everyone in the North shared these opinions.

After Abraham Lincoln issued the Emancipation Proclamation, which came into effect on January 1, 1863, any thoughts that the Civil War *wasn't* about slavery were quickly dispelled.

141

Massachusetts abolitionists allied with freedmen and freed Blacks in Massachusetts and other states to create an all-Black Union Army regiment.

The 54th Massachusetts Infantry Regiment wasn't the first Black regiment in the Union Army, but it was the most famous and effective. The soldiers of the 54th Massachusetts proved to the people of that era that Black soldiers could follow orders, stand strong in the face of fierce battle, and function as an effective fighting unit. Since the Civil War, the 54th Massachusetts rightfully earned collective hero status throughout the United States.

Ethnic Regiments

In the Civil War, the infantry regiments of both armies were generally formed at the state level. In the North, where immigration from Ireland, Scandinavia, and the German speaking kingdoms increased drastically before the war, ethnically-based regiments also became common.

The 15th Wisconsin Regiment was primarily made of Norwegian immigrants, the 8th New York Regiment was comprised of German-speaking soldiers, and the 90th Illinois Regiment was Irish, just to name three examples of many. These types of units were primarily in the Union Army, although the Confederacy had some German and Irish units.

So it was natural that some White abolitionists came up with the idea of creating a Black regiment.

The first experiment with a Black regiment in the Union Army was the 1st Kansas Colored Regiment. The 1st was formed in August 1862, more than a month before the Emancipation Proclamation was issued and several months before it went into effect; and was done so against the wishes of Secretary of War Edwin Stanton.

But Kansas was a border state and the war in the border states was largely partisan, and often guerilla in nature, so Stanton allowed the 1st to continue its unorthodox existence.

After the Emancipation Proclamation was issued, though, Stanton authorized Massachusetts governor John A. Andrew to muster a Black regiment. Stanton's efforts were supported by Boston's wealthy White abolitionist community, who bankrolled the recruitment efforts, with notable Black abolitionist Frederick Douglass (we'll get to him later) leading the recruitment effort.

Douglass and other recruiters traveled throughout the North to gather a diverse coalition of runaway slaves, freedmen, and Black men who were born free. They all wanted to prove their capabilities and fight for their and others' freedom in the South. It didn't take long to recruit enough men to reach the 1,000 needed for a regiment, but there was one thing...all of the officers had to be White.

As people of their time, even the White liberal abolitionists didn't have a problem with the provision that officers of the 54th had to be White, but they wanted one of their own to lead the operation. Captain Robert Gould Shaw, who came from an influential Boston abolitionist family, was promoted to colonel, becoming the man who would lead the 54th into battle.

Fighting for Their Freedom on and off the Battlefield

From the outset, Shaw and his men faced incredible odds from all sides. Confederate President Jefferson Davis issued a proclamation on December 23, 1862, that stated any Blacks fighting in the Union Army, and their White officers were considered in rebellion and therefore under an immediate death sentence if captured.

The 54th knew it wouldn't be easy, but they marched South on their mission.

As they faced the very real prospect that many, or possibly all of them, may not return from the South, the soldiers of the 54th also had to face discrimination from their own army.

Recruits to the 54th were promised $13 a month, the same as White recruits in the Union Army, but once they arrived in South Carolina, on the eve of their first engagements, they were disheartened to learn that they would only be paid $7 a month.

Today, when faced with a similar situation, many would probably just up and leave, and most people wouldn't blame them, but part of what made the 54th Massachusetts collective heroes is how they handled this situation. Yes, they protested and Colonel Shaw did his best to go through the proper channels, but ultimately, the men of the regimented decided to ignore the reduced pay *and* fight.

And fight the 54th did!

After being involved in some minor engagements in South Carolina, often in a support role, Shaw and the 54th were called upon to lead the charge at the Second Battle of Fort Wagner on July 18, 1863.

The 54th fought bravely, fearlessly assaulting the deeply entrenched Confederate positions that were not only on higher ground, but also protected by a series of trenches and parapets. The fighting raged for hours and when the smoke finally cleared the Confederate had the victory, just barely.

For Shaw and the 54th, the Second Battle of Fort Wagner had mixed results.

Shaw was killed in the battle and 270 of his men were either killed, captured, wounded, or missing. Although the 54th continued to fight in the Civil War, it was a shadow of its former self.

Perhaps the most important effect the Second Battle of Fort Wagner had for the 54th Massachusetts was the level of respect the soldiers gained, from the Union *and* Confederacy.

People in the North realized that Blacks soldiers could not only fight as well as their White counterparts, but they were just as patriotic and invested in preserving the American Union. After Fort Wagner, the Confederacy recognized Black

Union soldiers as enemy combatants and therefore eligible for POW status if captured, although this was not always followed by Confederate officers.

Ultimately, the 54th Massachusetts showed the country what was possible and that sacrifice and bravery know no boundaries.

DID YOU KNOW?

- The most notable member of the 54th Massachusetts was Sergeant William Harvey Carney. Carney was born a slave but escaped through the Underground Railroad to Massachusetts, where he then joined the 54th. During the Second Battle of Fort Wagner, Carney was wounded but carried the American flag over the ramparts, saying after the retreat that, "The old flag never touched the ground!" In 1900, Carney received the Medal of Honor for his actions at the Second Battle of Fort Wagner, and although he was not the first African-American to be awarded the Medal of Honor, the event that earned him the medal was.

- The 1989 film *Glory* chronicled the formation and life of the 54th through the Second Battle of Fort Wagner. Matthew Broderick played Colonel Shaw and Denzel Washington played Private Trip, who was based loosely on Sergeant Carney.

- Although former slaves comprised a sizable number of the men of the 54th, most were born free in Massachusetts and other Northern states.

- A large sculpture monument to the 54th Massachusetts was erected on the edge of Boston Common in Boston in 1884. It was the first monument in the United States that commemorated African-American soldiers and was somewhat ironically vandalized during the protests and riots against racism during the summer of 2020.

- Shaw was initially buried by the Confederate soldiers in a mass interment with his men in South Carolina. After the war, all of the men's bodies were disinterred and they were reburied at the Beaufort National Cemetery in Beaufort, South Carolina.

CHAPTER 21

JOMO KENYATTA: THE FATHER OF MODERN KENYA

As we've seen in our book, heroes and heroines are people like the rest of us, complete with all the flaws and frailties of humanity. Heroes can be polarizing, controversial, and sometimes downright scoundrels, so what then makes them special?

Some of the heroes profiled in this book had special talents, while others had a unique ability to see the world differently, but what made all of them influencers, and heroes and heroines long after their deaths, was the courage to meet a great challenge, or multiple challenges. For some, that involved rebounding from devastating losses, whether that was in politics, war, academics, or sports.

For others, it was about being at the right time and the right place in history and changing its course.

Jomo Kenyatta was one such hero. Often mired in controversy and haunted in his later years by corruption, Kenyatta was truly a complex leader. On the one hand, he was an anti-colonial pan-Africanist who worked towards the interests of a greater Africa, but on the other, he could be petty and provincial. He usually took an anti-communist stance at a time when developing countries often cozied up to the communist bloc, further adding to his seeming complexity.

Kenyatta worked hard to resolve problems between Kenya's different tribes and constantly sought reconciliation between the nation's Black majority and White minority, but he remained aloof and sometimes hostile towards Kenya's Indian minority.

Jomo Kenyatta was no saint, but he was the father of Kenya's independence. He may not have been the hero Africa wanted, but he was the hero that it got.

Born with Charm

Jomo Kenyatta was not born with his very distinct and regal-sounding name. Kenyatta was born simply with the name Kamau in a Kikuyu village in central Kenya (at the time the British Kenya Colony) sometime in the 1890s.

Village life was slow and easy for Kamau, who only spoke his native Kikuyu and some Swahili for most of his childhood. Wanting to see more of the world, in 1909, when he was in his teens, Kamau left his village to attend a Christian missionary school.

The missionaries who ran the school made all of the natives take Christian names after their baptisms, so Kamau chose Johnstone Kamau.

But the name never really meant much to Kamau, nor did religion. It was all a stepping stone towards what he would become years later. He would later take the name Jomo Kenyatta because it sounded more Kenyan and African.

Kenyatta never really did very well in his course work. Although he passed his classes, he did not distinguish himself academically. The missionaries didn't think Kenyatta would do much with his life, but they severely underestimated the young man's tenacity and charisma.

Kenyatta moved to the bustling city of Nairobi in the late 1910s, where he found himself working several odd jobs. He worked as a construction contractor, sold livestock, and served as a retail clerk. He was successful in all of his jobs, saving enough money to marry, start a family, and live a very nice life by native Kenyan standards.

Jomo was a "hustler" in the truest sense of the word, always looking for a way to "flip" something and make a good deal; and his charisma was a major asset to closing such deals.

Both of those traits would prove to be invaluable for Kenyatta when he began his political career.

Kenyatta reluctantly entered politics in the 1920s, joining the pro-Kikuyu group, Kikuyu Central Association (KCA), where he made invaluable contacts and learned the ways of Western politics.

As Kenyatta rose in prominence in the KCA, he was invited to speak to groups throughout Europe. He first went to England in 1929 but spent nearly two decades traveling throughout the continent. Kenyatta met with notable anti-colonialists from a variety of different countries, including Kwame Nkrumah, and rubbed elbows with some notable Marxists and communists, which earned him more than a few political enemies in Britain.

As World War II raged and then ended, Kenyatta had to make some important decisions. He had to decide what he was going to do when he returned to Kenya. Many of his people had fought and died for the Allies during the war, so he believed that it was only right that they should be given independence or at least control over the colony.

In 1946, Jomo Kenyatta decided to return to Kenya to lead his people to freedom.

Change Was Inevitable

By 1946, it was clear that change was inevitable and it was very likely that Kenya would become independent at some point. The British government could no longer afford to keep its empire and, after India achieved independence in 1947, it was just a matter of time before the rest of the major colonies in the empire went their own ways.

For Kenya, there were a couple of options.

There was the option of a more or less peaceful transition like the one that took place in India. The Kenyan African Union, later known as the Kenyan African National Union (KANU), favored working with the British to ensure a relatively peaceful transition.

Another option was favored by some in the White minority. Many Whites in Kenya saw South Africa and Rhodesia as ideal government models, whereby only Whites would control the government (as in South Africa), or with very limited Black participation (Rhodesia).

The final option was a bloody anti-colonial race war. This was the least popular option, even among the Kenyan nationalists, but it was popular with a large enough segment of the native population that it presented a real threat to stability.

In 1952, Kenya was thrown into the third option when the Mau Mau Uprising overtook the land.

Despite publicly denouncing the Mau Mau Uprising, the British authorities arrested and imprisoned Kenyatta in 1952 for supporting the rebellion.

Today, historians generally believe Kenyatta had nothing to do with the Mau Maus and was only imprisoned as a scapegoat and to show White Kenyans that the government was doing something. The Mau Mau Uprising was finally defeated by 1960 and conveniently Kenyatta was released in 1961.

Kenyatta's imprisonment only served to make him a national hero.

One of the most amazing things about Kenyatta's life, and what made him a hero in many people's eyes, was the fact that he harbored no ill will towards the British after his release.

Much like Nelson Mandela decades later in South Africa, Kenyatta extended an olive branch to the White Kenyan community and was willing to look to the future. Kenyatta also continued to work with the British government, keeping a lid on potential violence.

Kenyatta became the leader of KANU in 1961 and when Kenya finally became independent in 1963, he was the nation's first prime minister and later that year became Kenya's first president.

Unfortunately, Kenyatta let the power get to his head, becoming a dictator who violated his people's human rights. Despite the negative aspects of Kenyatta's later life, he is today regarded by many Africans as one of their top heroes for fighting for Kenyan independence, African unity, and by proving that major political change doesn't always have to be violent!

DID YOU KNOW?

- Jomo Kenyatta had four wives and eight children. Although a Christian, Kenyatta followed east African tradition by practicing polygamy. His most controversial wife, though, was a British woman named Edna Clarke.

- Unlike many anti-colonial leaders of the era who took socialist and pro-communist bloc geopolitical positions, Kenyatta firmly supported the West and only flirted with Marxism, socialism, and communism as a young man.

- Kenyatta gave amnesty to the Mau Mau rebels who continued to hide in the forests after the British suppressed the rebellion. He also tried to integrate them into the newly independent Kenya but with limited success.

- Kenyatta was a true Anglophile, having a life-long affinity for Britain and most things British, including food, literature, and clothing. He preferred modern, Western clothing to his traditional tribal garb.

- Jomo Kenyatta was a true capitalist who courted international investment and tourism as a major part of his economic policy. Some economists believe that Kenya's current position as a more economically successful sub-Saharan nation can be traced back to Kenyatta's economic policies.

CHAPTER 22

ALEXANDER BUSTAMANTE: BRINGING JAMAICA INTO THE MODERN WORLD

The struggle against colonialism and imperialism took many forms. Sometimes it took a violent turn, as we've seen with the Mau Mau Rebellion, but by the late 1950s, most independence leaders followed the example of Gandhi in India—independence from British rule appeared inevitable and could be done without violence.

As we've already seen with Kwame Nkrumah and Jomo Kenyatta, by the early 1960s, the question in many British colonies wasn't *if* most of these colonies would become independent, but *when* and *how*. Nkrumah and Kenyatta set the template for independence in Africa and although both men had many faults, they are considered heroes today for navigating their nations through their first years of independence.

In the Caribbean nation of Jamaica, Alexander Bustamante was the hero who guided his nation to independence. But as important as Bustamante was in the global anti-colonial struggle, he was very different from Nkrumah and Kenyatta, and Jamaica is very different from Ghana and Kenya.

If you just go by pictures, Alexander Bustamante doesn't look Black. His mother was of mixed European and African descent and his father was Irish. Under British colonial rules, and the social mores of the Caribbean at the time though, his African ancestry meant that Bustamante was legally Black and was considered as much by his fellow Jamaicans.

Bustamante also had a very different background from Nkrumah and Kenyatta. Unlike the two African leaders, who had well-documented backgrounds and were educated in European style schools, little is known about Bustamante's early life.

Jamaica was also quite different from Ghana and Kenya. Yes, Jamaica is a Black nation, but its Caribbean location meant that it developed quite differently to its African counterparts.

Jamaica doesn't have the tribal divisions that Ghana and Kenya have and its relatively close location to the United States and Latin America meant that it was influenced by those countries as much, if not more, than it was by Britain.

Truly, Jamaica was a different kind of country when the British Empire collapsed, so it needed a different kind of hero who would guide it into independence. Alexander Bustamante proved to be that hero.

A Mysterious Man

Just like the pirates who preceded him, Alexander Bustamante was a true son of the Caribbean, mysteriously moving from island to island while projecting an image that was larger than life.

Although much of Bustamante's early life is a mystery, it's known that he was born William Alexander Clarke on February 24, 1884, to Robert and Mary Clarke in Hannover, Jamaica.

Unlike the other national leaders profiled in this book, Alexander wasn't enthralled with Marxism, capitalism, or any other ideology for that matter.

He never claimed to be an academic and only had a grade school level formal education.

But like some of the other national leaders we've met, Bustamante was a charismatic individual from a young age.

Standing about 6′5, he was a physical presence in any room he entered, but he was never intimidating. Bustamante was known for being gregarious, magnanimous, and always welcoming toward all guests.

Young Alexander was also quite athletic, training and riding horses as a pastime and for some extra money in his youth.

I know what you're thinking: If he was born Alexander Clarke to Anglo-Caribbean parents, how did he get the Spanish surname "Bustamante"?

Bustamante later claimed that he took the name in honor of a Spanish sailor who brought him to Spain where he was educated as a boy. There's no evidence that Bustamante ever left Jamaica during his childhood, but there's plenty of evidence that he traveled throughout the Caribbean and Latin America from 1905 to 1934.

Alexander lived in Cuba and Panama during that time and visited several other countries.

As he worked as a policeman in Cuba, it is believed that is where he began using the Bustamante surname to better blend in with the Spanish-speaking natives of the island.

Making up an elaborate story, moving to another country to learn the language and culture of the locals, and even adopting a more culturally appropriate name in the process? It all certainly fits Bustamante's larger-than-life persona!

From Labor Activist to National Hero

When Bustamante returned to his native land, the world was changing quickly. Communism and fascism were threatening to envelop Europe and both ideologies also had plenty of adherents outside of the continent. In Jamaica, the organized labor movement was slowly becoming the de facto independence movement, which was led by mixed-race individuals like Bustamante and his cousin Norman Manley.

Ever the clever and enterprising individual, Bustamante saw what was happening and took advantage by forming his own labor union—the Bustamante Industrial Trade Union (BITU) in 1938. As arrogant and conceited as it may have seemed for someone to name a trade union after himself, it proved to be a boon to Bustamante's political career. Bustamante knew the Caribbean and his people in Jamaica in particular. He knew that Jamaicans respected bold men with big personalities, and as he had predicted, as the union grew, so too did his political profile on the island.

But the British weren't so happy with Bustamante's big personality.

The British authorities arrested Bustamante for provoking subversive, anti-colonial activities, holding him in prison for 17 months. But just as prison only helped to raise Jomo Kenyatta's anti-colonial profile, it also helped Alexander Bustamante's political career.

Bustamante left prison a household name and a hero to the Jamaican people.

In 1943, Bustamante founded the Jamaican Labour Party as the island's primary independence party. In 1944, the British decided to allow the Jamaican people universal suffrage, giving the island a degree of autonomy that the African colonies weren't afforded.

It was still a colony, though.

Jamaica's road to independence throughout the 1950s was a lot more peaceful and orderly than what took place in many other British colonies. Bustamante's cousin, and at the time political rival, Manley, advocated for the creation of a country that would be known as the Federation of the West Indies. It was envisioned as an Anglo-Caribbean federation, but when Bustamante said no, the Jamaican people followed.

Finally, in 1962, Britain granted Jamaica its independence in somewhat of an anti-climactic end to its anti-colonial struggle. Bustamante became the nation's first prime minister, holding the position until he retired in 1967.

The fact that Jamaican independence came with almost no violence and very little controversy cannot be understated and is considered by many to be a testament to Bustamante's negotiating and organizational skills. Bustamante brought his country peaceably into the modern world and for that he was named a "National Hero" of Jamaica, joining a very small and select group.

DID YOU KNOW?

- Bustamante was married four times but had no children. He married his fourth and final wife in 1962 when he was 78!

- Bustamante also became the prime minister of Jamaica in 1962 when he was 78; quite old for a head of state, but far from the oldest.

- Sir Arthur Richards was the governor of Jamaica who had Bustamante arrested in 1942. Though Bustamante was generally a thorn in the British government's side at that point, the specific incident for which he was arrested was a fiery speech he gave to a group of longshoremen in Kingston's port.

- Bustamante also served as the mayor of Kingston, Jamaica's largest city and capital.

- Alexander Bustamante died on August 6, 1977, in rural Surrey County, Jamaica at the age of 93. His body was interred in Heroes Park, Kingston.

CHAPTER 23

JACKIE ROBINSON: ERA-DEFINING HERO

Like it or not, professional sports are a major part of modern society. They've evolved from little more than a part-time pastime into a multi-billion dollar, global industry. Football/soccer is the most popular sport in the world, played in every country, with its many professional leagues generating billions in revenue. Professional basketball, hockey, and baseball are also global industries and although

American football is only played and followed on a major scale in North America, it too is a multi-billion dollar industry.

So there's no doubt that sports bring in a lot of dough for the athletes who play the games as well as the league and club owners,. However, sports can also change the way people view themselves, their neighbors, and the world.

We saw how Pelé is arguably the greatest Black football/ soccer hero in history, and perhaps the greatest Black athlete of all time, for his incredible feats on the pitch *and* his ability to bring people together from diverse backgrounds.

In the United States, there have been many Black athletes who brought together different and sometimes opposing people under the banner of fandom, just as Pelé did.

Track and field star Jesse Owens comes to mind for winning four gold medals at the 1936 Summer Olympics in Berlin, Germany. Owens did this feat in the face of the Nazi regime and at the height of the Jim Crow laws in the United States.

Few people doubt Owens' hero status, but the sport of track and field isn't a professional sport followed by millions of people. Because of that, the impact of Owens' career wasn't as great as someone playing a major professional sport.

So if you're searching for the greatest Black American sports hero, and arguably the greatest Black sports hero in the world next to Pelé, then you don't have to look any farther than Jackie Robinson.

Robinson was an incredible athlete, a true gentleman, and barrier-breaking hero. After becoming the first African-American to play Major League Baseball in 1947, Robinson showed the country that he was more than just a novelty or a political ploy, putting up incredible career stats on his way to being voted the National League rookie of the year in 1947, Major League All-Star six times, the 1949 National League MVP, and being inducted into the Baseball Hall of Fame on the first ballot in 1962.

Robinson was able to accomplish these stats even though segregation was still the law of the land in many states and discrimination was still common. His performance on the field and how he dealt with adversity off it made him not just a Black hero, but an American national hero. The number he wore during his Major League days - 42 - is the only number that's been retired by every Major League team.

Jackie Robinson changed not only how the game of baseball looked but also how it was played by introducing speed where before teams almost solely relied on power hitting. For all of these reasons, Jackie Robinson was a man who defined an era of sports and history.

The Power of Sports

The influence of sports on modern society can't be denied. We all know that playing sports can positively benefit a person's health, but they also have more wide-ranging and profound impacts on individuals and even for entire countries.

Jackie Robinson was one of those rare individuals who used his love and natural aptitude for sports to change the world.

Robinson was born in 1919 in racially segregated Georgia but grew up in Southern California after his father left the family. During the 1920s and '30s, California was also segregated, although not by law.

Jackie's mother Mallie worked hard to raise him and his four older siblings, but things weren't always easy. For a time, Jackie was a troublemaker on the streets of Pasadena, but then he was saved by the power of sports.

And Jackie wasn't the only talented athlete in the family. Jackie's older brother Mack won a silver medal in the 200-meter race at the 1936 Summer Olympics. Mack proved to be a constant source of inspiration for Jackie throughout his life and helped to steer him away from crime and delinquency and into sports.

Young Jackie excelled in football, basketball, baseball, and track and field. Basically, in any sport he played, he was the best on the field.

Robinson's athletic abilities earned him a spot on UCLA's football team in the early 1940s, where he was only one of four Black players. It would be the first of many barriers that Jackie would break and it helped prepare him for the added pressures of being one of the first and only Black players on future teams.

But as his college career began taking off, the Japanese bombed Pearl Harbor.

Robinson answered the call to fight for his country and in doing so was faced with the stark reality of legal segregation for the first time in his life.

While serving in the Army, Robinson became friends with another African-American sports hero - Joe Louis. The men combined their forces to petition for more Black officers. Although Robinson was promoted to lieutenant, he found himself facing a court-martial when he refused to give up his seat on a bus to a White officer.

Robinson was found not guilty of insubordination, although the incident marked the end of his military career. Jackie was newly married and about to start a family, so he didn't want to build a career in the military. He knew his true talent was in sports and if he wanted to make money, that was the route to follow.

Jackie Robinson also knew that in sports he may have a chance to make some serious changes to society.

Doing What Comes Naturally

When World War II ended, Jackie decided to take his talents to the professional sports leagues. He was so talented that he could've played just about any professional sport other than hockey or soccer - although he probably could have played those sports as well if he'd had time to learn them. In the 1940s *the* sport in America was baseball. Professional football and basketball just weren't what they are today, so Jackie set his sights on baseball.

But there was one major problem - the "Major Leagues," the American League and National League, weren't open to Black players.

Some Hispanics played in the Major Leagues, but for an African-American such as Jackie Robinson, his only option in 1945 was to play in the Negro leagues.

Jackie played for the Kansas City Monarchs of the Negro American League, but he always looked forward to a day when he could play in the Majors. Not only was the pay better in the Majors, but the competition was the best. If you could make it in the Majors, then you were truly one of the best players in the world.

It's important to note that although the 1940s was the era of Jim Crow in the United States, there was no law prohibiting Blacks from playing in the Majors. It was more a psychological barrier imposed by the leagues' owners, but one that Jackie believed he could overcome.

Robinson thought that if he trained hard and had a little bit of luck, he could earn a spot with a Major League club. He knew that it wouldn't be easy, but he was aware of the hurdles involved from his time at UCLA.

So when Jackie was offered a chance to try out with the Brooklyn Dodgers in 1945 by general manager Branch Rickey, he jumped at the opportunity.

Robinson played for a season in the Dodgers' minor league system before being called up in 1947 when he made history by becoming the first African-American to play in the Majors.

He received some pushback by Major League players and some fans, but also from Negro League players. Some Negro League players thought he wasn't the best among them and others should have been in his place.

Incredibly, despite all the distractions on and off the field, Robinson was able to put up incredible numbers his rookie year on way to winning the National League Rookie of the Year award.

He was also able to win the hearts and minds of the tough Brooklyn fans and those of his teammates on his way to becoming a civil rights hero to Black people around the world.

DID YOU KNOW?

- Jackie's birth name was Jack Roosevelt Robinson. His middle name was in honor of former President Theodore "Teddy" Roosevelt.

- Robinson was an infielder who spent most of his time at second base. He compiled an impressive .311 lifetime batting average and a respectable 137 home runs and 734 runs batted in for an infielder who only played in the Majors nine years (1947-1956). He played for the Dodgers for his entire Major League career.

- Jackie married Rachel Isum in 1946. The couple had met while they both attended UCLA in 1941. They remained married until Jackie's death in 1972. The couple had two sons and one daughter. The couple's son, Jackie Junior, died in a car accident a few months before Jackie died of a heart attack at his home in North Stamford, Connecticut. Jackie was 53.

- In addition to changing the racial composition of Major League Baseball, Jackie Robinson is also often credited with shifting how the game is played. Robinson was a prolific base stealer, sometimes referred to as the "father of modern base stealing." This wasn't a major part of the game before Robinson's career. In the decades since Robinson, every successful Major League team has had at least one notable base stealer on its roster.

- Robinson was also an early example of the "jock turned announcer," doing live color analysis for televised baseball games in the 1960s.

CHAPTER 24

LENA HORNE: BREAKING BARRIERS IN MUSIC AND FILM

As Josephine Baker made her mark in France, other performers were attempting to do the same thing under different conditions in the United States. No one can blame Baker for leaving the United States, especially when she received the offer she did, but most African-American musicians had to do their best at home.

Lena Horne was one such musician.

At first glance, Horne seems to have been born with a silver spoon in her mouth. She was exceptionally attractive, musically talented, and came from a middle-class family. All of that was fine, but in 1930s America, a Black woman still had to jump some extra hurdles just to be successful.

Although Lena Horne was of mixed European and African ancestry, and could in some cases "pass" as White, she was still Black according to the "one drop rule" in North America at the time. Because of that, Horne had many doors closed in her face and her roles in some films were even occasionally edited out for certain audiences.

Still, Lena persevered and became one of America's best known and most talented entertainers of the mid-20th century. Lena Horne recorded more than 40 full-length jazz and pop albums, several singles, and performed for live audiences around the world. She was also a familiar sight on the Silver Screen at a time when very few African-Americans were in films.

As laws and attitudes change in the United States by the late 1960s, Horne picked up more mainstream acting roles and even starred opposite White actor Richard Widmark in the 1969 western *Death of a Gunfighter*. Perhaps because Horne had a light complexion and relatively European features, the role didn't raise too many eyebrows across the country, but it was still one of the first American feature films to depict an interracial couple.

Horne used her celebrity in the 1960s to support the Civil Rights Movement and by the 1970s she was well-loved by Americans of all backgrounds. Many scholars believe that Horne did just as much to break down barriers in the American entertainment industry, and the wider society, as many full-time civil rights activists because her charm and good looks lowered many people's guards and helped them look beyond their prejudices.

Lena Horne was also the first in a long line of multi-talented female African-American entertainers. Long before Beyonce, there was Lena Horne!

Playing the Cotton Club

Lena Horne was born into an upper-middle-class African-American family on June 30, 1917. The Horne family boasted of teachers, entrepreneurs, skilled workers, and even an inventor among their ranks, so Lena's father Edwin "Teddy" was a bit of a disappointment.

Teddy was a gambler who was heavily involved with the Harlem criminal underworld, which got him into plenty of legal problems with the police and other problems with his peers. After a fair amount of turmoil, Teddy left the family when Lean was just three.

Horne moved around for most of her childhood, living with her grandparents in Atlanta, Pittsburgh, and eventually back to New York. No matter the circumstances, Lena always had a good attitude and was never a problem for her grandparents, but she was quite independent at an early age.

It was also obvious to those who knew her that she had a natural talent.

Lena could sing and dance and had that "it" factor required to make it in show business. Horne knew that she was destined for great things in her life, so she went where any young talented Black 16-year-old girl in New York would go: the Cotton Club.

The Cotton Club was an interesting place and in most ways uniquely American. It was a true jazz club that featured live music and chorus line dancing. Nearly all of the musicians were Black and the chorus line dancing girls were also Black, although they tended to be mixed and/or with light complexions.

However, the audience was entirely White – 'no ifs, ands, or buts about it!' Black people could perform in the Cotton Club, but only Whites could be customers.

And the customers were also a unique mix of American elites. Some of the top politicians and businessmen frequented the Cotton Club and rubbed elbows with well-known gangsters such as Dutch Schultz. Since the customers were among the East Coast elite, the price of admission was high and the performers were paid quite well. If you could land a gig at the Cotton Club, it was often the first step in a great career in the entertainment industry.

While working at the Cotton Club, Horne began performing with big band legends such as Cab Calloway. By the 1940s she was recording albums *and* getting roles in Hollywood.

Money, Fame, and Dignity

Throughout the 1940s and '50s, Lena Horne was *the* African-American actress in Hollywood. Granted, there weren't a whole lot of roles for Black actors at that time in Tinseltown, but if a script called for a Black actress who could sing and dance—which most movies of that era required—Lena Horne was usually a finalist for the role.

Despite the fame and money she acquired from Hollywood, Lena was often discouraged by the limited roles she was offered and disheartened by the ones she did get, as she saw them as stereotypical and sometimes even degrading.

So she returned to her nightclub roots in the late 1950s, but within a few years, the cultural tides were turning.

Horne played several nighttime variety shows of the 1960s, including *The Ed Sullivan Show* and *The Dean Martin Show*. These appearances on variety shows during the 1960s introduced Horne to an entirely new, younger crowd. Although they preferred rock n' roll, this audience appreciated her authentic style of jazz and pop.

Lena also used her fame to pursue causes she believed were important. She became friends with First Lady Eleanor Roosevelt, met President John F. Kennedy just before he was assassinated, and took part in the March on Washington for Jobs and Freedom on August 28, 1963.

When Lena Horne passed away on May 9, 2010, at the age of 92, she was remembered as a phenomenal entertainer who broke barriers and blazed paths for later generations. Perhaps most importantly, Lena Horne is revered as a heroine who never forgot her past but was always looking toward the future.

DID YOU KNOW?

- Horne played a USO show for Black US servicemen and German POWs. The Black servicemen were seated in rows behind the German POWs, so instead of doing her act on the stage, she performed in the middle of the crowd, facing the Black servicemen with her back to the German POWs.

- Horne was married twice. Her second husband, Lennie Hayton, whom she married in 1947, was Jewish. Needless to say, even in the more liberal entertainment industry and in the more liberal cities of New York and Los Angeles, the marriage was a bit risqué at the time. She had a son and a daughter with her first husband, Louis Jordan Jones.

- Lena Horne won four Grammy Awards, although they all were awarded either late in her career, or after she had retired.

- In addition to her Grammys, Horne won several other awards, but the most prestigious was a Tony Award she won in 1981 for *Lena Horne: The Lady and Her Music*.

- Horne's left-wing politics temporarily landed her trouble during the 1950s, getting her branded a communist and temporarily blacklisted from Hollywood. After disavowing communism, she was removed from the blacklist and returned to acting.

CHAPTER 25

SHAKA: KING OF THE ZULU NATION

There are some names and words that just seem to have a certain amount of power. When you say them, you know you are saying something powerful, almost like saying a spell or an ancient incantation. "Shaka" is one such name.

You've probably heard the name Shaka at some point in your life and noted it for its cool sound. You maybe even know that it was the name of a famous person or even a king.

Did you know, though, that Shaka was the king of the Zulu Empire who earned that position through some pretty ruthless means?

Shaka was born in July 1787 into Zulu royalty in what is today called South Africa, but things were never easy. He was essentially cast aside as a bastard and had to join a military unit with all the other young, able-bodied men. That could've been the end of Shaka's story, but he had big dreams and ideas for the future of his people.

The young Zulu warrior rose through the ranks of the Zulu military until he ran the show. But instead of just sitting back at that point and getting fat, as countless other chiefs had done before him, Shaka unified the Zulu's into a cohesive fighting unit. Shaka also introduced fighting tactics that made his army unbeatable against other Zulus and - once he unified the Zulus - unbeatable against other African tribes. After Shaka was assassinated in 1828, the Zulus continued to use his military tactics, even against the modern weapons of the Boers and the British, giving them a run for their money.

Due to his successful efforts to unify the Zulus and the introduction of new fighting methods, Shaka was remembered by Black South Africans during the apartheid era as a hero and freedom fighter. Shaka's legacy was violent, but there's no denying that he was among one of the most important Black heroes in military history, right up there with Toussaint L'Ouverture and Taharqa.

Not Exactly a Silver Spoon

As mentioned above, Shaka was born Shaka kaSenzangakhona into Zulu royalty to King Senzangakhona, but that didn't necessarily entail an easy life. Although Shaka was the son of a chief, his mother was far down in the pecking order of the chief's wives, which relegated Shaka to a lower status. Shaka was raised by his mother in *kraals* (Zulu pastoral village) while his half-brothers lived in relative luxury at their father's court.

Once he became a teen, Shaka became an impi (warrior), as all able-bodied young Zulu men were expected to do. Shaka distinguished himself on the battlefield as brave and skillful against other Zulus, but more importantly, the young warrior learned a thing or two about politics.

The Zulus may not have had the same political structure as Europeans did in the 1800s, but they did have one. The Zulus practiced a form of government that was a mix of absolute monarchy and war-lordism: There was an official dynastic line, but weak leaders were routinely challenged and sometimes assassinated. The Zulus were also comprised of several different clans or tribes with many different chiefs. Before Shaka, there was no single Zulu chief or king who could unite all the clans for any extended period.

When Shaka was in his late twenties, he had his first chance to challenge the system. After Shaka's father died in 1816, one of his brothers took the throne. This was challenged by another Zulu chieftain named Dingiswayo, who just happened to be Shaka's father figure.

Shaka was then in the middle of the first truly chaotic situation in his life as the various Zulu clans and other local tribes fought each other in a bloody civil war.

Shaka's surrogate father Dingiswayo was killed during the civil war by a man named Zwide, who led the Ndwande tribe. Normally the death probably wouldn't have warranted much concern, as death was something that came with the territory of being an impi, but Shaka took Dingiswayo's death personally.

So personally that he devoted much of his time and energies to finding Zwide and when he did, Shaka had the chieftain killed in a very slow and painful manner.

Shaka had Zwide locked in a hut with some hungry hyaenas, which proceeded to tear him apart from limb to limb.

The vicious execution marked the end of the war between the Zulus and the Ndwande, which ended with Shaka's victory and the realization of his empire around the year 1819. Despite being outnumbered by as much as five times, Shaka was victorious due to numerous reasons, which we will now explore.

New Ways of Waging War in Africa

Perhaps what makes Shaka a true hero is not necessarily his bravery on the battlefield, although he distinguished himself in that regard, but more so what he did before the first spear was ever thrust in a battle. Before Shaka, warfare in southern

Africa consisted of quick battles done by small units, where few men died and minimal land changed hands. After Shaka, battles where hundreds of men on both sides became more common; although, with the greater number of warriors came a greater number of casualties.

But Shaka is also often credited with introducing diplomacy to southern Africa.

Shaka made many of his early gains by bringing smaller Zulu clans into his empire peacefully. By offering these chieftains cattle, grazing lands, and other spoils of war, Shaka was able to unify the Zulus against the Ndwande.

Shaka also introduced new tactics and weapons that essentially modernized the Zulu army.

The Zulus had fought much the same way for centuries before Shaka came to power, so his success in getting them to change their methods is yet another example of Shaka's diplomatic abilities as well as his charisma.

Perhaps the most important change Shaka made to the Zulu military was the introduction of the "bull horn" formation. This was essentially a pincer movement, whereby the elite impis would be placed in the center of the formation, drawing the heaviest of the enemy's attack. The less seasoned impis would comprise the horns, which would slowly encircle the enemy. Reserves were kept in the back to make sure that none of the enemy escaped alive.

Shaka also standardized the weapons of the Zulu army. He substituted longer spears for the short stabbing spear known as the iklwa and introduced larger, heavier cattle skin shields.

Despite all of the work Shaka put into building a great empire, he was unable to rule it for very long. In 1828, his half-brothers had him assassinated so they could rule the vast empire. Although treachery is what ultimately brought Shaka down, he had a hand in his own demise. When his mother died the previous year, Shaka became unhinged and despotic and ordered the execution of thousands of his people he deemed to have failed to be sufficiently grief-stricken.

Needless to say, this erraticism didn't sit well with the Zulus.

Although Shaka experienced a rather unheroic death, he lived his life as a hero and a champion for his people. Because he left his people in a stronger place, he will always be remembered as one of the premier Black military tacticians and political leaders of world history.

DID YOU KNOW?

- Although the South African National Congress (ANC) was not specifically a Zulu ethnic organization, it incorporated an image of an iklwa into its logo, as it was the symbol of a strong Black kingdom that resisted colonial rule.

- Since the Zulus didn't have writing or photography, most of the modern depictions of Shaka's physical appearance are based on oral accounts. Shaka was described as tall, lean, and muscular, but not particularly good looking.

- At its height, the Zulu Empire probably numbered around 250,000 people.

- Shaka's forcible unification of all Zulu tribes and the defeat of non-Zulu peoples led to a period of migration known as the Mfecane. Some non-Zulus went north, while others went west and south, sometimes conflicting with the British and Boers.

- Shaka forbade his warriors from marrying until they had sufficiently proven themselves in battle. It also appears that he never married nor had children.

CHAPTER 26

REDD FOXX:
THE ORIGINAL KING
OF COMEDY

Before Chris Tucker, there was Chris Rock and before Chris Rock, there was Eddie Murphy. And of course, before Eddie Murphy, there was Richard Pryor, considered by many to be the number one Black standup comic of all time.

But before Richard Pryor hit the stage with his manic routines that combined observational comedy with "blue" humor,

John Elroy Sanford, better known by his stage name, Redd Foxx, toured America doing standup comedy and making studio albums of his routines, which due to the era were sometimes difficult to find.

If you're reading this and were born in the 1970s or earlier, or a fan of classic American sit-coms, you probably know Foxx from his hit television show, *Sanford and Son*.

Foxx brought his routine to a much wider audience through that show, making Americans laugh and blush with his combination of physical humor, bawdy and occasionally racial jokes, and of course his enduring catchphrases.

"Lamont, you big dummy!"

"How would you like five across your face?"

And of course: "I'm having the big one. Elizabeth I'm coming to join you!"

During his career, Foxx broke barriers by being one of the first Black comics to play to predominantly White audiences in Las Vegas. By the '70s, he showed Americans that despite some of our problems, or maybe because of them, we can still sit back and laugh at each other.

Like many of the heroes in our book, Redd Foxx was in many ways the product of his time and also a reflection of it. He challenged social issues in his comedy and inspired generations of comedians to follow in his footsteps and brought people together from diverse backgrounds in laughter.

Many heroes achieve their status through conquest, while others do so by challenging laws or even helping make them, but Redd Foxx conquered millions of peoples' hearts and minds with some clever jokes and plenty of physical humor.

A Winning Personality

It's not easy to be a professional comedian. For every major star you see on HBO or some other premium cable channel, there are hundred more toiling away in comedy circuits around the country. For every one of those hundreds of comics nominally working in the industry, there are thousands more who can't get their feet in the door.

This was no different for John Sanford in the late 1930s and early 1940s.

Sanford was born on December 9, 1922, in St. Louis, Missouri but was primarily raised on the south side of Chicago.

After Sanford's father left the family when he was a child, causing him and his older brother, Fred Junior, to find male role models elsewhere. Like many people placed in difficult situations, Sanford also used humor to deal with the breakup of his family.

And it was immediately clear to everyone who knew John, that he was a true comic.

John had a naturally gregarious nature, an excellent memory, and a quick wit, which helped him become a comic legend. As he went through school and worked different odd jobs as a teenager and young adult, he often practiced his routines on his friends, family, and coworkers.

He was always a hit!

So, you're probably wondering, how did John Sanford get the name Redd Foxx?

Well, as a child and young man, he was often called "Red" due to his complexion and hair color. Since his mother was racially mixed, Sanford had a lighter complexion and a slight tint of red to his hair. In parts of the American South and within the African-American community at the time, people with Sanford's background were often referred to as "Redbone," which was abbreviated to Red. When Sanford made it big, he just added a "D" to go along with the name "Foxx."

Sanford took the name "Foxx" as an homage to his favorite baseball player, Jimmie Foxx. It was later said that Sanford used two "Xs" in his last name to denote the blue nature of his act, but the truth is that he was a really big baseball fan and loved to watch Jimmie Foxx play.

By his late teens, Foxx knew that he had the talent and desire to make it big, but that he'd have to go to New York to do so.

The Big Time

In the late 1930s, New York City was the place to go if you wanted to make it in the big time of the entertainment industry. Films were being made in Hollywood, but there was no television, and the music industry, stage, and what was left of vaudeville were all based in New York.

So that's where Redd went.

Foxx got his foot in the door playing in a band called the Jump Swinging Six. The Six played live radio gigs and in nightclubs, even in the legendary Apollo Theater. But the pay was lousy and the gigs were too infrequent for Foxx to make a living.

So, after a while, he listened to the advice of some friends and decided to give the relatively new art form of standup comedy a chance.

Foxx landed on what was known as the "Chitlin Circuit" in the 1940s and '50s. The Chitlin Circuit was the comedy circuit played by Black comics for Black audiences throughout the East Coast, South, and Midwest.

The Chitlin Circuit was known to be a bit bawdier ("blue" as it's called in the comedy business"), borrowing heavily from the African-American word game known as "the Dozens," whereby individuals make fun of each other with clever putdowns often done to rhymes.

Redd found immediate success on the circuit and sometimes toured with a childhood friend named Slappy White, calling their act "Redd and White."

Foxx's reputation on the Chitlin Circuit preceded him, leading to him getting more and bigger offers. Finally, jazz singer Dinah Washington saw Foxx perform on the East Coast and convinced him after the show to take his talents out West.

Foxx met with Dootsie Williams, owner of Dootsie Records, and the rest as they say is history.

Dootsie signed Foxx to his record label and arranged for him to do the more lucrative Vegas circuit.

Always busy, when Foxx wasn't doing live performances, he was in the studio making albums. Foxx recorded more than fifty LPs during his career and many more singles, compilations, and collaborations.

By the time Foxx passed away in 1993 at the age of 68, he was a comedy legend in his own time. Most standup comedians were influenced by Foxx in one way or another and nearly every Black comedian saw him as a hero for breaking down barriers so they could shine.

DID YOU KNOW?

- Foxx's first comedy LP was titled *Laff of the Party*. Although a hit that spawned several sequels and proved to be the launching pad for Foxx's career, it only earned him $25. Foxx sold over 15 million records during his career but later blamed Williams for taking most of his money through carefully worded contracts.

- Foxx was married four times. Although Fox had no children of his own, he adopted his second wife's daughter.

- Despite making millions during his long career, he constantly had money problems throughout his life. He constantly lived above his means, even for a millionaire, and ended paying his first three wives millions in spousal support and divorce settlements. In 1989, the IRS seized Foxx's Las Vegas home and most of his personal property for owing nearly one million dollars in unpaid taxes.

- When Foxx was scraping by trying to make a name for himself in New York City in the early 1940s, he met legendary Black activists Malcolm X. The activist referred to Foxx as "Chicago Red, the funniest dishwasher on this earth," in *The Autobiography of Malcolm X*.

- Foxx died of a major heart attack on October 11, 1991. The heart attack came while he was filming a scene for the sitcom in which he was currently starring, *The Royal*

Family. Because Foxx was a prankster off-screen, and due to his character of Fred G. Sanford in *Sanford and Son* often faking heart attacks, many on the set initially thought he was joking.

CHAPTER 27

FREDERICK DOUGLASS: FROM SLAVE TO ABOLITIONIST

The institution of slavery has existed since the dawn of human civilization more than 5,000 years ago and probably much earlier. It is likely that the earliest humans, living in caves and other primitive settlements, practiced a form of "situational" slavery whereby they took captives during violent exchanges with other clans.

The reality is, though, that slavery as a system is a byproduct of the civilized world. This may seem like an oxymoron, but it's true.

As human societies became more complex and developed in terms of governments, division of labor, and economics, slavery came to play an increasing role in many of these societies. The type of slavery changed from society to society, ranging from serfdom to indentured servitude and chattel slavery, but many societies were still practicing a form of it until the 1800s.

The United States was one of the last countries in the Western world to abolish slavery, but it was the only country that fought a war that ended the practice. The debate over slavery in the United States was bitter and divisive, yet despite it ultimately concerning the lives and futures of millions of Black people, it was for the most part a conflict between Whites.

Those who supported slavery were White, but even the vast majority of the abolitionists were also White.

There was one notable exception—Frederick Douglass.

Frederick Douglass was so much more than a Black abolitionist, though, as he was born a slave, taught himself to read, and eventually made the perilous journey to the North and freedom. Once in the North, Douglass found that his race still limited him in certain situations and that although slavery may have been illegal north of the Mason-Dixon Line, racial discrimination was very legal and sometimes very ubiquitous.

Like many of the heroes and heroines in this book, Douglass preserved and continued to fight to end slavery. His anti-slavery campaign eventually brought him recognition and fame beyond the shores of America, leading him to search for allies in the fight against slavery in Ireland, Great Britain, and Canada.

After slavery ended, Douglass continued his activism by supporting the women's suffrage movement and writing about his ideas, observations, and experiences in several books.

There's little doubt that Frederick Douglass was one of the most influential Americans in the 19th century and that he played a major role in the end of slavery in the United States. Frederick Douglass is certainly a hero for that alone, but the way he accomplished so much makes him even more of a hero. Douglass was always willing to listen to others, even those he vehemently disagreed with, and he believed that violence should only be used as a last resort.

Becoming Frederick Douglass

Frederick Douglass was born into slavery in the Chesapeake Bay region of Maryland, possibly in 1818, although due to poor recording keeping for slaves at the time the exact year is unknown. He was named Frederick Augustus Washington Bailey, taking the surname of his mother, who was a slave of predominantly African descent. His father was White, possibly his mother's owner. The unfortunate reality is that

Frederick never really knew his father *or* mother. He was taken from his mother when he was an infant and primarily raised by his grandmother, who was a slave, and maternal grandfather, who was free.

For those unfortunate enough to be born into slavery at the time, the conditions covered the spectrum from humane and even somewhat enlightened to awfully brutal.

Young Frederick experienced the complete spectrum.

When he was six, Frederick was sent to live with a White couple in Baltimore. He later wrote that conditions for urban slaves were notably better than those experienced on plantations. Urban slaves were usually domestic workers or skilled artisans and were often given much more freedom than their counterparts on large tobacco and cotton plantations. Frederick also learned how to read while he lived in Baltimore.

Frederick was then sent to live with the Auld family, which proved to have its ups and downs. Thomas Auld, who was Frederick's actual owner, proved to be a tyrant, but Frederick lived with his brother Hugh and Hugh's wife Sophia for several years. Sophia taught Frederick the basics of reading, which meant that when Hugh later forbade her from teaching Frederick anymore and forbade Frederick from reading, the young slave was able to continue his education by himself in secret.

Later, to teach his brother and the apparently recalcitrant Frederick a lesson, Thomas sent Frederick to a farmer known for treating slaves cruelly. Frederick was relentlessly beaten until one day, at the age of 16, he decided to fight back.

It proved to be a profound turning point in Frederick's life.

The farmer never again beat Frederick.

As Frederick continued to live under servility, he was inspired when he met free Blacks in and around Baltimore. One of those free Blacks was a woman named Anna Murray, who helped him escape to freedom.

Murray used her knowledge of ferries, trains, and roads that went to the North to help Frederick travel to freedom. Once he safely made it to freedom, the couple reunited in New York and married in 1838.

They then changed their surname to "Douglass" and the famous abolitionist activist Frederick Douglass was born.

Leading the Fight against Slavery

After gaining his freedom, Douglass could have lived a relatively worry-free life in Massachusetts with his wife and family. He could have chosen any number of professions to enter and would have been protected by the fairly significant abolitionist communities in Massachusetts and New York.

But instead, Douglass chose to be a very public activist, which put his life and liberty in danger once the Fugitive Slave Act of 1850 was passed.

Douglass began his career as an abolitionist by preaching in Black churches in New York and New England, which is how he developed his superb oratorical skills. He also wrote his own sermons, helping him improve his writing abilities.

In the 1840s, Douglass had many significant connections within the abolitionist community throughout the United States and traveled extensively to support the cause. He was greeted with sympathy in many places throughout the Northeast, but often harassed and even beaten in the Midwest (at the time, the Midwestern states of Indiana, Illinois, Michigan, etc. were known as the "Northwest). Things weren't easy at this point in Douglass's life and career, but he persevered.

Eventually, Douglass gained fame in Europe and was invited to speak to many individuals and organizations in Ireland and Great Britain.

The tour proved to be a success on many levels. First, it allowed Douglass to spread his "brand" to a much greater and sympathetic audience. Second, it showed Douglass how things could be without slavery, although also how poverty can still exist in a society without slavery. Finally, and perhaps most importantly, he came back from Europe with plenty of money donated by wealthy benefactors.

Douglass used the money to publish the abolitionist newspaper *The North Star*. *The North Star* was the premier abolitionist paper of the period until it merged with *Liberty Party Paper* in 1851, creating the *Frederick Douglass' Paper*, which then became the leading abolitionist paper.

But by the mid-1850s Douglass knew that America was on a collision course over the slavery issue that probably couldn't be stopped. During the 1850s Douglass promoted dialogue and diplomacy with the other side, even as the rhetoric became more heated and violent.

But it was getting more difficult every year for those invested in the issue, such as Douglass, to avoid conflict. He befriended radical White abolitionist John Brown, and although he didn't support Brown's violent actions, he agreed with him in theory.

Once the war began, Douglass helped recruit for the Massachusetts 54th Regiment. Once the Emancipation Proclamation was made and the war was over, Douglass shifted his activism to focus on the women's suffragette movement.

When Frederick Douglass died at his Washington, D.C. home of a heart attack on February 20, 1895, at the age of 77, he was still working non-stop for the causes he believed in. He had given a speech in favor of women's suffrage just that day. Douglass is remembered as one of the leading forces in the abolitionist movement and was a living example that a former slave could become an educated, articulate, and refined leader of men.

DID YOU KNOW?

- Douglass wrote and published three autobiographies: *A Narrative of the Life of Frederick Douglass, an American Slave* (1845), *My Bondage and My Freedom* (1855), and *The Life and Times of Frederick Douglass* (1881). The third book is more comprehensive as it relates many details that could have put his family in danger before the Civil War.

- Douglass thought that President Abraham Lincoln was too moderate, so he supported Radical Democrat John C. Freemont for president in 1864.

- The Washington home of Douglass, located at 1411 W Street, SE, in the Anacostia neighborhood of the city, is a national historic site administered by the National Park Service.

- Douglass had five children with Anna. After Anna died in 1882, Frederick remarried a White abolitionist named Helen Pitts in 1884. Although the Pitts family were notable abolitionists, they disapproved of the interracial union and cut off ties to Helen. Frederick's children also disapproved of the marriage.

- In 1899, a statue of Frederick Douglass was erected in Rochester, New York, making him the first Black man to have such an honor in the United States.

CHAPTER 28

GASPAR YANGA: AFRO-MEXICAN SLAVE LIBERATOR

When you think of Black history in the Americas, the countries that come to mind tend to be the United States, the Caribbean nations, and Brazil.

There is good reason to think that way, since these were the primary destinations of African slave populations and where the largest populations of Blacks in the Americas developed.

You probably don't think of Mexico as a top destination of African slaves, but for a time, New Spain, as Mexico was called when it was ruled by Spain, had 200,000 slaves, making it one of the highest slave populations in the Americas.

Today, most of the Mexican population is mestizo—a mixture of indigenous and European ancestry - but just over 1% of the population has significant African ancestry and identify as Black or Afro-Mexican. Most Afro-Mexicans today are descended from African slaves brought to the colony - primarily in the state of Veracruz, but also in some of the coastal Pacific coastal areas - from the 16th through early 18th centuries.

The life that African slaves faced in New Spain was a bit different from what they experienced in British North American (what would become the United States), as mixing with other ethnic groups took place more freely, although the brutality directed against them was just as, if not more, frequent.

The African slaves of New Spain found themselves in what seemed to be a hopeless situation, but in 1570 a man named Yanga, who claimed to be a prince from a region in Africa that is now Gabon, offered many slaves a way out: He would lead them to safety and freedom in the highlands outside of the city of Veracruz.

Hundreds followed Yanga into the mountains where they attempted to build a community separate from the Spanish.

Nearly 40 years later, in 1609, the Spanish located Yanga's colony and attempted to drive the former slaves from their mountainous camp, but the Africans were ready. Fierce fighting followed, which eventually ended in a tactical stalemate but a strategic victory for Yanga, as he was allowed to have his colony.

Because Gaspar Yanga led one of the only successful slave revolts in history, and because he followed the military victory up by establishing a new community where former African slaves could live in peace and harmony, he is remembered as a hero in Mexican history and for Black people around the world.

Becoming a Maroon

At some point in your life, you've probably heard the term "maroon" used as a verb, or possibly you've used it yourself: "how did we get marooned here?"; "she was marooned with her boyfriend's family"; "the boat's crew was marooned on a desert island."

To "be marooned" means to be stranded somewhere, usually in an isolated location.

But the verb maroon is actually based on a noun.

From the 16th through the early 19th centuries, the trans-Atlantic slave trade was a major business in the Americas. The institution of slavery itself persisted into the mid-1800s in the United States and the late 1800s in Brazil. Therefore, the population of runaway slaves grew to large numbers in some places during this time. Some of these runaway slaves formed isolated communities and became known as "maroons."

It was a big change for an African slave to run away. As bad as slavery may have been, it brought a certain amount of stability. Slaves knew they were fed and cared for to a certain degree under the system, so running away from it brought many hazards and they had few options once they did run. Stealing a ship to go back to Africa was impractical if not impossible, so they could only hope to go deep enough into forests, jungles, and/or mountains to avoid the authorities.

Many of the runaways perished. Those in the more northern climates of North America had to contend with cold weather and topography, flora, and fauna with which they were unfamiliar. Those closer to the equator fared better, but they also had to contend with many unforeseen risks.

All runaways had to deal with the native and First Nations populations they encountered.

Sometimes those encounters were violent, in which case the Africans usually came out on the short end of the stick, but often the Africans formed new communities with Indians they met, which became maroon communities.

This was the historical and cultural backdrop that Yanga had to contend with in 1570.

Little is known about Yanga's background other than that he was originally from a region of west-central Africa that is now Gabon and that he was given the Spanish first-name "Gaspar." Modern statues depict him as lean and muscular, which may be correct since it would take an imposing man to lead such a mission.

Yanga was said to be a skilled orator and quite charismatic, as he was able to convince dozens or more slaves to give up their unfree yet stable lives for uncertainty and danger in the Veracruz highlands.

As time went on, Yanga's colony grew, accepting more and more former slaves. They survived through a combination of agriculture, trade with the local Indians, and robbing Spanish authorities and merchants.

Eventually, as the Spanish presence in New Spain grew as well, the Spanish authorities decided to do something about Yanga's colony of maroons.

War with the Spanish

When compared to other slave revolt leaders and revolutionaries throughout history, Gaspar Yanga was quite conservative. By the time the Spanish sent a force of more than 500 soldiers to put an end to Yanga's maroon colony in 1609, Yanga was quite old and no longer able to lead his people on the battlefield. Still, he was their leader and sent a message to the Spanish that he was willing to negotiate.

Yanga wanted a basic peace treaty whereby both sides agreed to leave each other alone. Yanga even agreed to return any future runaway slaves to the Spanish.

But the Spanish wanted nothing short of total capitulation.

The ensuing fighting was fierce and bloody, lasting for several years. The Spanish burned Yanga's settlement, but the maroons

simply established a new one farther in the mountains, and then they went on the counteroffensive with a series of guerilla attacks on Spanish caravans and outposts.

The maroons finally achieved victory when the Spanish agreed to most of Yanga's demands, with the added proviso that Yanga's family would essentially rule the community as a dynasty.

Yanga's maroon community was eventually absorbed peacefully into the state of Veracruz, but he is remembered today as an important freedom fighter in Mexican and world history.

DID YOU KNOW?

- After making peace with the Spanish, the maroon town of San Lorenzo de los Negros de Cerralvo was officially established. Today that town is known as Yanga, Veracruz.

- Yanga was posthumously honored by the Mexican government in 1871 as a "national hero of Mexico" and the "first liberator of the Americas."

- The most common year of birth given for Yanga is 1545, although this isn't known for sure.

- The locals of Yanga hold a festival every year to celebrate Gaspar Yanga. A bronze statue of Gaspar holding a machete and spear was designed by Erasmo Vásquez Lendechy and erected in the town of Yanga in 1976.

- Although Yanga came from what is today Gabon, most Afro-Mexicans can trace their ancestry to what is now Angola and other parts of southwestern Africa.

CHAPTER 29

LANGSTON HUGHES: LEADING THE HARLEM RENAISSANCE

Earlier in this book, we discussed how hardships produced the blues and how B.B. King and other notable bluesmen used their experiences to become world-renowned music artists. This was also true of the careers and lives of most of the men and women we've explored in this book—the trials and tribulations of their lives made them the people they became.

Nelson Mandela probably wouldn't have become South Africa's first post-apartheid president if he hadn't spent all that time in prison.

Frederick Douglass probably wouldn't have become one of the most influential abolitionists if he hadn't first been a slave.

Shaka probably wouldn't have become the king of the Zulus if he hadn't been pushed out of his father's home and forced to make his own way.

Struggles can destroy many people - physically, mentally, and spiritually - but those who overcome them often become stronger. We've seen how many of the heroes and heroines in our book fought against struggles, which were often legal or social barriers, and sometimes used them to define their lives and even a generation.

Langston Hughes used the struggles of African-Americans to produce some incredible poetry and other writings that define Black American culture in the 1920s and '30s. Through his unique observation abilities and his loquacious pen, Hughes was able to articulate the struggles as well as the hopes and aspirations of millions of people who were often overlooked in American society.

Hughes' writings played a central role in the era of American history known as the Jazz Age, helping to spur the Harlem Renaissance of the 1920s. This was when the Harlem section of New York City became ground zero in great cultural, political, and economic changes and advances that were taking place within African-American culture. The Harlem Renaissance would have long-lasting ripple effects throughout African-American culture, influencing the Civil Rights Movement as well as later forms of Black culture.

At the center of the Harlem Renaissance was Langston Hughes, who countless Black artists and activists from later generations viewed as a pioneering hero.

A Restless Soul

Like any writer worth their salt, especially a poet, Langston Hughes was a bit of a restless soul. Born James Mercer Langston Hughes on February 1, 1901, in Joplin, Missouri, Hughes moved around with his family a lot in Missouri, Kansas, Illinois, and Ohio.

From a young age, Hughes, or "Langston" as he preferred, had a true affinity for words and language. He constantly put his observations down on paper, but instead of those words being dry prose, they jumped from the pages alive with energy.

Langston landed a spot at the elite Columbia University in 1920, but he faced two problems: He was one of only a few Black students and Columbia and New York were expensive.

After appealing to his estranged father in Mexico for financial support, he was able to enroll at the university as long as he studied engineering as his father wanted. But Langston soon found that engineering wasn't his thing and despite proclaiming to be a racially progressive institution, Columbia rarely lived up to its reputation.

So Hughes did what any good writer would do and hit the road.

Hughes made Harlem his home base in the 1920s, and for the remainder of his life, but traveled the world extensively in the '20s and '30s. He served in the US Navy in the early '20s, which brought him to Europe and Africa, giving him a different perspective on politics and race. Hughes was part of a group of young African-Americans to visit the Soviet Union in 1932 and he later visited China, Japan, and other east Asian countries in addition to traveling throughout the Caribbean and Latin America.

All of Hughes' travels certainly gave him grist for his writings, but it was his experience as a Black man that was at the core of his art and what made him famous and even revered in some corners of society.

The poem that launched Hughes' career - and some would say the Harlem Renaissance - was his 1921 work "The Negro Speaks of Rivers." The poem was first published in the National Association for the Advancement of Colored People's magazine, *The Crisis,* and later republished in a 1926 anthology of Hughes' poetry titled *The Weary Blues.*

The publication of the "The Negro Speaks of Rivers" caused a sensation among the African-American community because it was so different from anything that had come before it, yet it seemed to speak directly to the often-tired souls of so many. The poem tells the story of the Black man throughout world history as he struggled to find meaning and a sense of identity.

Meaning and identity were at the center of all Hughes' works.

By the 1930s, Hughes' had written and published dozens of poetry anthologies, a dozen novels and short stories, children's books, plays, and later, several nonfiction books. Hughes always stayed true to the idea of exploring the struggles of the Black race on the one hand, and on the other hand, their latent power.

Hughes was an active writer and activist until his death in 1967, but in the years before his death, quite a few things had changed. Some on the New Left saw Hughes as being too nationalistic in his racial views, while some Black nationalists, such as the Black Panthers, thought Hughes was too conservative.

In the end, though, serious Black writers all admired Hughes for blazing the trail that allowed them to be successful. Maya Angelou may be a better remembered African-American writer, but she and others from her generation owe a debt of gratitude to Langston Hughes.

DID YOU KNOW?

- In addition to his work as a poet and fiction writer, Hughes wrote columns and articles for several newspapers. In 1937, Hughes traveled to Spain to cover the Spanish Civil War for the *Baltimore Afro-American* newspaper.

- Hughes befriended and worked with many other luminaries of the Harlem Renaissance, including painter Aaron Douglas. Where Hughes' work captured the trials, tribulations, and victories of Blacks in words, Douglas' did so through paintings. Hughes and the other writers and visual artists of the Harlem Renaissance preferred to represent subjects from the lower classes of the socio-economic ladder.

- Although Hughes family tree was quite racially mixed and he, therefore, was lighter in complexion, he preferred to portray the lives of darker toned African-Americans. At the time, lighter-skinned Blacks tended to control the economics and politics of their communities, so Hughes meant to challenge that control in many of his writings.

- Hughes never married nor had any children.

- Hughes earned a BA from the famous HBCU Lincoln University in 1929, although he was already a famous and successful writer at the time. While he was offered many teaching and lecturer positions throughout his life, he only accepted to teach at Atlanta University in 1947 and as a visiting lecturer in 1949 at the University of Chicago Laboratory Schools.

CHAPTER 30

KALEB OF AXUM: PROTECTING EARLY CHRISTIANS

Our study of great Black heroes and heroines began with the last emperor to rule Ethiopia, Haile Selassie, so it's fitting that we end with one of the first great rulers of Ethiopia - Kaleb of Axum.

Kaleb was the emperor of the ancient and medieval Ethiopian kingdom of Axum in the early 500s CE. He is best known for being a conqueror and protector of some of the world's oldest Christian communities.

As a conqueror, Kaleb extended Axum's territory from encompassing what is today Ethiopia, Eritrea, Somalia, and most of Sudan to also include what is now Yemen, making the kingdom a true empire where a diverse range of different ethnicities and religions could be found.

But when it came to religion, Kaleb was a devout Christian.

A major reason why Kaleb extended Axum's territory into the Arabian Peninsula was to protect Christians who were being persecuted there by Jews. Once Kaleb successfully conquered Yemen, he showed great tolerance and mercy by allowing the Jews of the region to continue practicing their religion.

For his efforts protecting early Christians on the Arabian Peninsula and for promoting Christianity in sub-Saharan Africa, Kaleb was venerated as a saint by the Egyptian Coptic Church, the Ethiopian Coptic Church, the Greek Orthodox Church, and the Roman Catholic Church. A majority of the Christian churches rarely all recognize a single saint, which makes Kaleb of Axum a great Christian and African hero.

Kaleb and Axum

The Kingdom of Axum, or sometimes spelled "Aksum," is so named for the city that served as its capital in northern Ethiopia for most of its history. After the various kingdoms of ancient Nubia, Axum was the next greatest kingdom in sub-Saharan Africa and eventually replaced Nubia for that title.

The exact date when the Kingdom of Axum formed is debated, although most scholars believe it was gradual, beginning sometime in the early 1st century BC.

By the 3rd century CE, Axum was starting to come into its own as a kingdom, and its distinct culture was beginning to take form. First, Christian missionaries began flowing into Ethiopia from Egypt. The Egyptians established Coptic churches and monasteries throughout Ethiopia and by the 4th century, the leaders of Axum accepted the Coptic version of Christianity.

It was also in the 3rd century that the kings of Axum first began flexing their military muscles. The Axumites conquered most of their smaller neighbors in northeast Africa before turning their attention north in the 4th century to conquer the Nubian kingdom of Meroe.

When Kaleb came to power in the 500's, he already had a wealthy and powerful empire at his feet, but the intelligent, crafty, and ambitious leader was ready to make it larger.

Protector of the Christians

Kaleb is known from several primary sources, including the writings of Greek Byzantine historians such as Procopius and inscriptions from Ethiopia in the ancient Ge'ez language. Unfortunately, there are no detailed biographical accounts of Kaleb, but what is written about the King paints the picture of a clever and pious ruler.

Kaleb maintained good relations with the Egyptians to his north and there is evidence that he met with an ambassador from the Byzantine Empire in CE 530. The evidence seems to suggest that Kaleb wanted to build better relations with the Christian world at the time, Egypt, the Byzantine Empire, and possibly the Christian kingdoms of the West. There's no doubt that Kaleb did this partially to enrich himself and his kingdom, but nothing says that he couldn't do that *and* promote Christianity in Africa, possibly with the long-term goal of building an ecumenical alliance.

Kaleb also used his unofficial title as the leader of Christianity in Africa to protect Christians in Arabia.

In the 6th century CE, the Himyarite Kingdom of Arabia was led by a Jewish king named Dhu Nuwas. Dhu was a powerful and expansionist king, who ruthlessly defeated all his enemies and repressed all religious opposition. Since this was about 100 years before Islam, for Dhu Nuwas, his primary religious opposition was from Christians.

Dhu Nuwas focused much of his communal wrath on the Christians of the city of Najran in southwestern Arabia. Nuwas was well-armed, well-funded, and organized, so the Christians put up little resistance, but they did get the word out to other Christians that they were in dire straits.

Only Kaleb and the Christian kingdom of Axum answered their call.

Kaleb used the situation in Najran as a *casus belli* to go to war and extend his kingdom into Arabia, but there is no doubt that his actions at least temporarily saved the Christian community in Najran.

After defeating Dhu Nuwas, Axum included most of what is today Yemen, making it an empire comparable in size to its contemporaries the Byzantine Empire and the Sassanian Empire. Although the Axumites weren't able to hold their gains in Arabia, Kaleb's war in Arabia made him a hero to all medieval Christians and African contributors to Christian culture.

DID YOU KNOW?

- The Ge'ez script that was first developed by Axum scholars more than 1,500 years ago is still used today in Ethiopia.

- Kaleb's successor was Alla Amidas. Many scholars believe that they ruled as coregents, with Alla Amidas taking care of things in Ethiopia while Kaleb was campaigning in Arabia.

- Little is known about Kaleb's family, but according to some sources he had a son named Gabra Masqal.

- Kaleb was venerated by the Catholic Church in the 1500s as Saint Elesban. Although he is venerated by all the major Christian churches since the churches all have different calendars, Saint Elesban has three different feast days.

- It is believed that Kaleb abdicated the throne in favor of Alla Amidas and then retired to a monastery, although details about the end of his life are sketchy.

CONCLUSION

I hope you enjoyed taking this journey through *The Great Book of Black Heroes: Thirty Black Men and Women Who Have Impacted History* and that you learned a few things in the process.

Among all the interesting facts that are crammed into this book, you probably knew before reading this book that heroes and heroines come from all backgrounds, races, and nationalities. Now that you've read this book, you know that, within the Black community, there has been an incredibly diverse amount and types of heroes and heroines.

Hopefully, you've learned a thing or two you didn't know about the more popular and well-known Black heroes such as Martin Luther King Junior and Harriet Tubman while having your eyes opened to lesser-known Black heroes like Taharqa, Gaspar Yanga, and Jomo Keyatta.

You've learned about great Black warrior leaders like Shaka and Toussaint L'Ouverture, Black scholars such as George Washington Carver and Frantz Fanon, and Black artists like Josephine Baker and Langston Hughes.

You've also learned that an African-American named Thomas Sowell has played a leading role in the American conservative movement.

To sum it all up, there isn't just one type of Black hero in world history. There have been many types of Black heroes and heroines throughout every age, in Africa, North America, the Caribbean, and Latin America who've contributed to their communities and the countries where they lived.

If anything, this book has shown that heroes and heroines are made when they rise above a challenge and set an example for others. The heroes and heroines of this book are remembered not just for what they did, but also who they were and the type of lives they lived.